To Claire + Thomas —

Good Friends;
Now that I am familiar with your skill at my ready...
I insist you come along next time.

Al

Out-of-the-Way Places

✦

Green Peas Don't Make Good Soup!

John Reynolds with Wade Swink

iUniverse, Inc.
New York Bloomington

Out-of-the-Way Places
Green Peas Don't Make Good Soup!

Copyright © 2008 by [John Reynolds with Wade Swink]

All rights reserved. No part of this book may be used or reproduced by any means, graphic, electronic, or mechanical, including photocopying, recording, taping or by any information storage retrieval system without the written permission of the publisher except in the case of brief quotations embodied in critical articles and reviews.

The views expressed in this work are solely those of the author and do not necessarily reflect the views of the publisher, and the publisher hereby disclaims any responsibility for them.

iUniverse books may be ordered through booksellers or by contacting:

iUniverse
1663 Liberty Drive
Bloomington, IN 47403
www.iuniverse.com
1-800-Authors (1-800-288-4677)

Because of the dynamic nature of the Internet, any Web addresses or links contained in this book may have changed since publication and may no longer be valid. The views expressed in this work are solely those of the author and do not necessarily refl ect the views of the publisher, and the publisher hereby disclaims any responsibility for them.

ISBN: 978-1-4401-0752-8 (pbk)
ISBN: 978-1-4401-1202-7 (cloth)
ISBN: 978-1-4401-0753-5 (ebk)

Printed in the United States of America
iUniverse ref. date: 11/04/2008.

Foreword

The following pages are a record of the nearly six weeks Wade Swink and John Reynolds spent exploring: exploring the back roads of the United States; exploring the upper reaches of Canada; exploring new ideas about the way the world works; and exploring what the future has in store for two old friends who have already lived most of their lives, but are still eager to see what lies ahead.

The writing is in the first person. This is an editorial convenience. The contents emanate from two separate journals we each kept along the way that I assembled and organized as best I could. Any misrepresentations are the fault of the editor for which, Wade, I apologize in advance.

John Reynolds

Introduction

I read lots of road trip books. Kerouac's *On the Road*, of course, and Steinbeck's *Travels with Charlie,* and Waugh's *When the Going was Good.* William Least Heat-Moon's *Blue Highways* and Larry McMurtry's book on interstate highways. Walking trips, too. Peter Jenkins' *A Walk Across America*, and more recently Rory Stewart's *The Places in Between.* And just about everything Bill Bryson has ever written.

There is something seductive about the idea of just hitting the road and seeing who and what you run into. No firm plans. No set itinerary. Perhaps a general sense of direction, nothing more. I was no stranger to this. In my youth I had wandered through Afghanistan and Pakistan. Later, at the age of 17, a friend and I spent several months roaming about Asia. In my 20s I had meandered around the Andes for a summer, and more recently revisited Europe with an only moderately structured itinerary.

But, despite many thousands of miles of driving around this country, the dream of a destinationless road trip around the United States was still just a dream. I had been talking about taking this kind of trip for a long time. I referred to it as my "Blue Highways Tour" after Moon's book about wandering the back roads (the blue highways) of America. I had read the book in the 80s and had rolled the idea around in my mind ever since.

My plan was not to travel completely alone. I would advertise the trip and invite friends along for various legs based on what parts of the country they had always wanted to visit. If Rick had always wanted to see the Badlands, he could join me, say, in Fargo, and we would tour the Dakotas. I would then drop him off in Sioux City and pick up Jim, who had never crossed the Great Plains…and so on.

But advertising was as far as things went, like pushing soap with no concrete plans to build a soap factory. It was just an attractive concept that I never tired of revisiting. Apparently my musings did not have the same effect on everybody else. After listening to me arrange and rearrange this trek for twenty years, most of my friends had long since decided that it wasn't going to happen.

Then I got an e-mail from an old friend from the Army, Wade Swink, who said, "I suggest we drive a stake into the ground relative to the blue highways trip."

We? All of a sudden *my* blue highways trip had become *our* blue highways trip. But he had a point. I had done a lot of talking, but had not gone much beyond that. Wade was no stranger to this sort of thing himself, and actually made things happen. He had just come back from an outing to the Outer Banks of North Carolina to try out his new camper (an old one actually, but with very few miles on it, and Wade is an engineer with a gift for making old mechanical things new again). A couple of years earlier he had driven up to the Arctic Circle by himself to take in the frozen sites for a month.

So, why not? Okay, I said. Then began the negotiations.

My vision was whipping down Route 66 in a reconditioned 1961 Impala convertible (a yellow one to be specific. I have been told that Chevy did not make a yellow one, but I have seen two of them with my own eyes so I can testify that somebody did.) A summertime excursion, I saw us stopping in old motels and bars at every opportunity and talking to everyone we met.

Wade's thoughts were a bit different. He proposed heading due north through Quebec to Hudson Bay sometime in October and November.

The difference may be partly attributable to our origins. Wade was from South Carolina, had spent his Army time in Viet-Nam, and had lived in Williamsburg, VA pretty much ever since. He liked and was used to "hot," so for him cold places spelled adventure.

I, on the other hand, had spent much of my time farther north and in mountainous places. Afghanistan for several years, high school in Cleveland, college in West Virginia, homes in Maine and most recently the mountains of Northeastern Pennsylvania. Cold weather was old hat for me, and my idea of an exotic getting away was Hawaii.

He wanted north; I wanted west. Northwest was the obvious compromise. We agreed to head up to Manitoba and Saskatchewan and come down through Montana and the Plains. The tour would have to wait until the fall, however. In July I was hosting my family's first reunion in 50 years, to be followed by a heavy schedule of volunteer work and then a family wedding the beginning of September. Fortunately, work was flexible—Wade and I were both "semi-retired" and scheduled our work at our convenience. We decided to aim for immediately after the wedding.

During the back and forth, we seized on polar bears in Churchill as a common goal and the furthest point of the trip. Routes to and from there would be determined day to day as we went.

Bear season in Churchill runs from mid-October to mid-November, when it is just about impossible to book anything in the tiny town. Not to mention you cannot actually drive there. The last several hundred miles must be navigated by train or plane, and they book up pretty tight.

Our goal was to be in Churchill sometime during the last half of September, when we could still find a seat on the train, a bed to sleep in, and a shot at spotting some white furry creatures. I also had to be back by the second week in October to host an event at a local museum. Other than that, no agenda.

Wade pretty much took it from there. Outfitting the camper, guidebooks, all that (did I mention he was an engineer?).

But, and it was a big "but," could two sexagenarians who, though they had been friends for 40 years, actually get along in a small camper for a month? Life-long friendships have been known to end this way, and that was a lot to put at risk. Better to put a toe in to test the waters first. We agreed to a trial run of three or four days in Ocracoke, a small island in the Outer Banks of North Carolina accessible only by ferry.

April in Ocracoke

I headed down to Williamsburg the last week in April, 2007. Wade and his wife Patty live in a tony golf course community on the James River called Kingsmill, next to Busch Gardens. He had been one of the early pioneers to build a house there 35 years ago when the Busch (Budweiser) folks opened up the development. I had a temporary contract with NASA Langley and was staying in the area at the time, so I had several tours of the work in progress. I was quite impressed with the details and the amount of work he put into it himself. It would be several decades before I had the confidence to try a similar project of my own.

Even though Wade and I had both trained as Army engineers, he was the real deal, with a degree in the subject. My fellow classmates and I had recognized his ability in Army Officer Candidate School early on when he was chosen as our first cadet commander and supervised some of our early bridge building. I, on the other hand, never quite got the hang of creating structures (one of my bridges almost fell into a ravine), though I did display some talent for blowing things up—the dark side of combat engineering.

Though I had been camping a number of times over the years, I had never been the man in charge. My style of traveling is to go pretty light, find a cheap hotel, and then walk the area from sunup to sundown, talking to as many people as I can along the way. Organizing sojourns in the woods (or, in this case, at the beach) was not one of my skills. Fortunately, there was always an old friend, or an uncle, who loved that part of the endeavor, so all I had to do was say "sure" when I received the invitation and follow the checklist I was given of things to bring and chores to do. My mom used to say I might not be much of a leader, but I was a darn good follower.

My North Carolina checklist was pretty short as Wade took care of almost all the logistics. My chief responsibility was providing the music. I come from a somewhat musical family and grew up listening to the classics. My father was especially fond of Wagner and Rachmaninoff and had hoped to be a classical pianist himself. When that didn't pan out he—naturally—became a journalist of sorts, but never quite gave up on the idea of a career in music. He would spend the rest of his life working on and off on an operatic adaptation of Poe's *The Raven*.

When I moved to New York in the early 60s Wade and Patty were two of my first visitors, so I introduced them to Broadway and later to the opera via La Boheme. For Wade it was love at first hearing and he became an instant opera fan. So, for this trip he charged me with bringing some of my opera collection and a battery-powered device to play them on. I carefully selected a dozen or so of my favorite operas, as well as some Broadway classics and several Sinatra albums for variety.

I got into Williamsburg late afternoon and enjoyed wine and dinner with the Swinks and a couple of their neighbors who drop in regularly. We left for the shore after breakfast the next morning. Our transport was a 26-foot 1993 Toyota camper that Wade had picked up cheap a few years before and painstakingly brought up to code. The front looked like a pick-up truck. The rest of it was wider than the front (double wheels on the rear axle) and hung over the passenger compartment. Above my head (I was generally in the passenger seat as Wade liked to drive and I am usually a happy passenger and don't press to drive other people's vehicles) was Wade's bunk, which stretched out a couple of feet on either side of the cab doors. Wade had warned me to duck down when I got out, but I was usually so eager to stand up that it took me quite a while to remember this even though I banged my head repeatedly. "Long learning curve" was how Wade put it.

We stopped for gas after several hours. The camper had a six cylinder engine and was pretty good on gas mileage for a camper I guess. Still, we had to stop every two hundred plus miles or so to tank up. I volunteered to do the pumping, jumped out of my seat, and bumped my head.

Several hours out Wade suggested that I treat us to some music. It was then that I realized that I had left all of the music behind in my car.

Things got quiet as we crossed from Virginia into North Carolina. There were some sidelong glances and a smirk. My failure to successfully complete my primary mission (opera) and my inability to make a graceful exit from the camper had already established me as the junior officer here. Not that I wouldn't have been anyway (it was his camper, after all, and he had done all the work). But, such a display of incompetence in such a short time could not help but evoke bemused condescension, however good natured. We stopped in Nags Head for a fast Chinese lunch. I was starving and leaped out of the camper. "Watch out..." Wade warned me too late. I bumped my head right on cue.

The Outer Banks had grown a lot since my last visit, with housing and commercial developments everywhere. In the early 70s when I had been a regular it had been much quieter, not to mention rustically charming, and I had even thought about buying a house on the beach. Fortunately a gregarious drunk at a local eatery had seen fit to ridicule the idea and lecture me on the shifting sands that are the Outer Banks (they are essentially a long ribbon of sand dunes jutting out into the Atlantic Ocean). My dream house disappeared under the waves some years ago. Even the Hatteras lighthouse, once a considerable hike from the oceanfront, had to be picked up and moved west lest it be washed away. Thank God for pushy sots.

We ferried across from Cape Hatteras to Ocracoke on a boat operated for free by the state of North Carolina, a trip I had made many times. A ten mile drive along a narrow two-lane highway with dunes and ocean on one side and Pamlico Sound and some wild ponies on the other brought us into the only town on the island, famous for being the site of Blackbeard the Pirate's last hurrah. The town was bigger than I remembered, but not by much. It's an easy walk from end to end and side to side in a couple of hours.

We checked in to the local campsite and found a spot close to the ocean in the furthermost corner. Wade backed into the spot and blocked the camper so it wouldn't rock. He then pulled out a folding table and some folding chairs and set up housekeeping. I didn't have much to do save for stowing my stuff in the little compartments I had been assigned and walking the endless beach on the other side of the dunes.

Wade had asked if I wanted a bicycle to ride. I had said no—I had lived on bikes when I was a kid and had never liked them then. When the world moved from English racer three-speeds to real racers with multiple gears, banana seats and handlebars below your knees, my distaste turned to hatred. Wade was an enthusiast, however, and was planning a cross-country bike trip. He is one of a number of my friends who think nothing of coming home from work and hopping on the bike for a quick 20-mile spin before dinner.

To be a sport, I got on one of the two-wheelers and took an awkward spin around the camp. "I've seen enough," he said, convinced that I would be a menace to society and a danger to myself if I were to venture onto the highway. He biked alone after that. If he was seriously disappointed he never let it show. His amusement, however, was hard to conceal, if indeed he even made the attempt.

That night he lit a fire and handed me some chicken to cook. We had wine, chicken, and salad and talked about…everything. That was the first indication I had that our road trip was to be about more than geography. I guess I should have realized it sooner. There is probably nothing unusual about a man who reaches the age of retirement, the time of life when many other men his age turn to the golf course and the pursuit of breaking 100 for their inspiration, and asks himself if life doesn't have more to offer. Wade could see many golfing role models every day just by stepping out his front door. He was never tempted to follow their example. "Golf is a good walk spoiled," he would say, quoting his father, who lifted the line from Mark Twain.

So here we were, two men of relative leisure with the time to examine what came before and what lies ahead and question it all. How am I doing so far? What should I have done differently? What should I do different now? Do my values still make sense? Did they ever? How much time do I have? What waits for me at the other end?

Maybe the last question was the big one for Wade, who had not paid much attention to religion most of his life, but who had in the past few years become quite curious about it. His wife and many of his neighbors had joined what had started out as a small church not so many years ago and had since grown into a megachurch by Williamsburg standards. Wade had been attending, but was not yet a member. He was, however, a frequent attendee and active in a church group that provided house repair services to the elderly and indigent. Fixing plumbing and repairing roofs was child's play for Wade, and doing it for those who could not do for themselves was rewarding. And Christian. And while he pounded nails, he pondered just what else Christianity actually meant.

Both my grandfathers had been ministers, one Episcopalian, one Baptist, though I had never known either of them. My mother raised us as Episcopalians, but my three sisters and I had wandered off. My oldest went through Southern Baptism and Roman Catholicism (including a stint in a convent) before settling in with some form of Islam. I had plans to become an Episcopal priest myself, but thought better of it by the time I was a junior in college. Since then, my associations with any church were generally in conjunction with a birth, a death, or a wedding. And that was it.

We traversed the subject of religion, recognizing that we would revisit it more than once in the coming weeks, and went on to politics.

Wade is a firm free-market Republican. I am a fallen away Democrat who was attracted to populism and independent candidates. Then on to science and history (Wade was deep into Thomas Jefferson and Lewis and Clark). And then we drifted into drowsiness and headed for bed. Bedtime on the road would usually come around 9, with a bit of preliminary reading, and then up with the sun.

A stiff wind came up and would stay with us for the next two days. It was so strong that Wade's attempt to light the water heater (a gas device on the side of the camper) proved futile, so it was to be cold showers. As long as the water was cold anyway, I chose the camp showers where the pressure was better.

Wade slept in the loft over the passenger compartment, while I took the foldout that ran lengthwise from the driver's seat to the kitchenette. I think I passed out right away and don't remember much until sometime in the middle of the night when I dreamed I was being trampled by a giant lizard (I loved monster movies as a kid growing up during the golden age of Godzilla and still dream of being attacked by a giant something or other from time to time). I woke to realize that someone was walking across my bed. The toilet was in the back of the camper, and the only way Wade could get there was by walking over me. He closed the thin sliding door, which blocked out the light but did little for sound. So I listened in for a few minutes until he plodded back over me and went back to sleep.

The third day out Patty came down to pick me up and bring their dog to keep Wade company for the next couple of days while he camped by himself and thought things through. Did he still want to go through with the month-long road trip? Did he think he could stand being cooped up with an absent-minded guy with such a long learning curve who wasn't even a Republican.

"I'll let you know," he said. Hardly the enthusiastic endorsement I had been fishing for, but this kind of commitment should be made with eyes wide open after careful consideration. While I was satisfied that I could deal with the close quarters and the novelty of it all—I go for the item on the menu I have never heard of and treat life much the same way—if Wade wasn't enthusiastic, the hell with it.

I spent a pleasant day driving leisurely back to Williamsburg with Patty where we went to her favorite Thai restaurant. Patty is one of those southern (South Carolina originally) charmers who makes a point of knowing everyone and being interested in what they are doing. Close as Wade and I have been over the years, we might have drifted away from each other but for his wife's skill in embracing people like me and making them feel like critical parts of her extended family.

I spent the next day catching up with old friends in the area and then went home to Pennsylvania to wait for Wade to make up his mind. Several days after returning home, and without any definitive statement from Wade, I started to receive a flood of information on polar bears, Churchill, and Canada in general. In the sales profession this is known as assumed consent. Never mind the formalities of an explicit agreement to go forward with the contract, just sign here and write me a check. So it was. No grade was forthcoming on my performance at the beach; we just advanced to the next level. While Wade is prepared to talk at length about almost anything else, interpersonal issues are often monosyllabic. "Okay" being his resolution to most things (actually, okay is two syllables), and "bye" his signal that the conversation is ended.

Worked for me.

I had a family wedding outside Cleveland the beginning of September. We agreed that he would pick me up there and we would head north.

September 9—Strongsville, Ohio

I partied at my niece's wedding Friday and Saturday. Wade appeared with his camper early Sunday morning ready to roll. We weaved our way through a throng of young boys in hockey uniforms (the ice rink was next door) and bigger boys dressed in Cleveland Browns sweatshirts (it was Sunday and there was a game downtown). We left Strongsville, Ohio around 10 a.m., headed into driving rain that would be with us most of the day, and took the interstate to Toledo and then north to Ann Arbor, Michigan.

From there we planned to take back roads to Fenton, Michigan, but somehow took a wrong turn and headed off on I-96 to Lansing. We backtracked and wended through the historic towns of Williamston and Howell, ending up in Fenton late afternoon. On the way we passed a stand with large plastic palm trees and "killer tomatoes," probably a reference to the classic horror movie.

We had a late lunch in Fenton at a place called the French Laundry. No sight of dirty clothes, nor of anyone who spoke French. We had some distinctly American fare: Wade had salmon in parchment and I had turkey meatloaf topped off with berry pie for dessert.

Sitting outside to enjoy the warm weather we talked about what constituted "historic" as we looked at the historic houses in historic downtown Fenton, noting that so much of the country was now classified as historic. It was getting hard to find a town that didn't have an historic district on the National Register of Historic Places. Some years ago I myself had been involved in establishing something called the Montrose Park Historic District. On a visit to Montrose, Scotland, I talked to the historic folks there who were amused to find that we considered anything 100 years old to be historic. Their town dates back to the 1100s. Now that's historical!

We also talked about Wade's nephew, who was off in LA pursuing an acting career (as was my nephew), and the number of other young people we knew who had dreams of show business or sports as careers. The subject of religion came up. I noted how many churches I knew that were sustained by a dwindling number of gray heads. Not so with Wade's, but there is something about advancing age that either stokes one's dedication, or rekindles it… or ignites it for the first time (to continue the metaphoric string) as it did with Wade. Perhaps for some of us it is what remains relatively unchanged and comfortable, or maybe it provides us with something to look forward to by turning to God as our time on earth grows short. No conclusions, but it would prove to be only the first of many discussions on God and church.

We camped for the night at Hickory Lakes (7 Lakes) State Park, which was an old borrow pit—a site where soil and rock was excavated for use somewhere else. The hole was now a lake with some campsites alongside. We pulled into site #32, which coincidentally was $32 a night, next to a family from Ann Arbor. They had two young red-headed boys, Jacob and Caleb, who biked around the campsite and begged their father to play "monster" with them. He told us he worked for ADP in Ann Arbor and said he was lucky—good jobs were getting scarce. He and his wife were full of suggestions about what we should see as we worked our way up north and along the coast of Lake Huron. Tawas Lighthouse was worth a stop and Mama Mia's pizza was as good a place as any in Mackinaw.

Later on the young (27) camp ranger stopped by to talk. He was finishing his master's in biology and was interested in birds. He was worried about his job and told us how bad the employment situation was in Michigan. We would notice ever more obvious signs of economic distress as we traveled through Michigan, reinforcing my own observations that the country was heading for a bad patch that might last a while. I had been expecting something big for some years now, but the experts kept saying the economy was sound. Curiously, the booming housing market was often held up as evidence, though it seemed to me to prove just the opposite. Having been trained as an economist myself, I had developed a healthy skepticism of economic forecasts, which, like so many prognostications, seemed to fall victim to what I have heard called the "sunny day" problem. In the field of meteorology, if you predict that tomorrow's weather will be like today's, you will probably be right more than half the time. A string of sunny days, however, would not alert you to a hurricane just over the horizon. Not surprisingly, many social prophets base their prophecies on historical data, so they are probably right more than half the time, but pretty much blind to a looming catastrophe that doesn't appear in the recent historical data. And they don't have satellite imagery to help them keep an eye on approaching economic storms. As for me, though, my tour of back road middle America had me worried.

September 10—Up the Lake Huron Coast

We woke up at 4:30 to lighted sky all around. I thought it was dawn, but there was some kind of mining operation that explained part of it, as the sky was overcast. It was warm; the temperature would climb into the 70s by afternoon.

There was a stretch of damaged homes on the way into Fenton. I had heard that a small tornado had touched down in Michigan a week earlier, and our route had taken essentially the same path as the twister. Tornados seem to be working their way north, part of global warming perhaps. I have been concerned about changing weather patterns and had insisted that any house I live in have a good solid basement to run to when killer winds threatened. Our house in Pennsylvania has a poured concrete basement built into the side of the hill.

We drove into Standish, following the signs to Wheeler's restaurant and bakery. One sign said since 1925, and another said since 1937. We learned while we were eating lunch—pretty good cabbage soup with a turkey wrap—that there were two places owned by the same person and that they dated from 12 years apart.

Wade and I talked about America's health insurance problem. As both of us are veterans with access to the VA health system (and Medicare not far off)—and are both in good health—the problem does not have the immediacy for us that it does for many. That does not mean that we did not have strong opinions. I had been in the health insurance business for some years, recognized that it was wasteful and obscenely expensive, and felt that affordable health care of some kind (I tend to favor public clinics) could be made available to everyone— and well should be given the amount of money this country spends on health care.

Wade is leery.... No, that's not quite right. Inalterably opposed to anything resembling universal health care would be more like it. His feeling is that if society provides everything, what encourages responsible action? "Just like welfare," he said, "universal health care will discourage responsibility in exactly the people who need to learn it the most. We have to put social programs in place that show compassion, but at the same time foster responsible action. Responsible action comes before respect." A worthy point, no doubt honed in discussions with his friends and neighbors in the medical profession, but worthy nonetheless. Still, I pointed out, considering how much we spend on health we ought to be able to design a better system that is within manageable reach of virtually all of our citizens.

We moved on.

After lunch we walked down a very, very quiet main street past a store that had lots of clothes hanging from the eaves. They were under the watchful eye of a very wary young woman. As the three of us were the only people to be seen anywhere, and there appeared to be no obvious miscreants about, I asked if she was really that concerned about thieves. She assured me that she was and looked us over carefully. At first I was a bit put off at the very idea that we might run off with any of her goods, but then I imagined what she might be thinking about a couple of unshaven needy-looking old guys in well-worn jeans. I cut her some slack. There was an orange rain parka priced at $8 hanging in the middle of the clutter of wearables—too good to pass up, I thought, though Wade managed to walk on by with no trouble.

I went in and plunked down my 8 bills. I wore my purchase proudly, but didn't impress Wade...or anyone else who saw me in it during the trip. Never mind.

On to the Tawas Lighthouse, another historic site that had come highly recommended by the couple at the campground. There was a sign that explained that the site had been surveyed by none other than George Gordon Meade, the hero of Gettysburg, as part of the Lakes Survey he conducted between 1856 and 1859.

We walked up to the top of the lighthouse with our cameras as well as one from a couple on the ground who had forgotten to take their camera when they went up earlier and who didn't want to climb again. (Actually, there were two couples, and only the husbands did the climb...once.) We tried to get them everywhere to look up at us from their bench seats down below when we took their picture, but no amount of screaming or banging on the windows could attract their attention. With $1 donations we bought badges to commemorate our ascent from a young woman who was assigned to sit up at the top of the lighthouse and was very happy to have company. I asked questions about the light itself, and the buildings below, but she couldn't answer any of them. Apparently her historic sensibilities—and curiosity—did not run deep. We walked back down and returned the camera to the waiting tourist couple, then got back in the camper and headed north again.

We had seen a lot of signs for smoked fish (apparently a local delicacy) along the way so we stopped in a grocery store and asked for some. The clerk pointed to some disappointing looking silvery-brown stuff in the case and said "that's all we have." I was sure that what we had seen advertised must be more interesting than that, but we bought it anyway and set off to the Long Lake campground near Alpena— about 90 miles south of Mackinaw—for the night. We paid $20 for a night at site #60. (Wade keeps meticulous records of such things. Did I mention he's an engineer?) We had the smoked fish with wine and cheese and listened to *Der Meistersinger* on the CD player. After my ignominious showing in Ocracoke I had plastered post-it notes with the word "opera" on them everywhere to ensure against a repeat performance. Wade was underwhelmed with both the fish and the cheese and said I could finish it all, which I did over the next several days. He did enjoy the wine and the opera.

September 11—Mackinac Island

Another rainy day, albeit unseasonably warm. We continued our drive up the Lake Huron shoreline to Mackinaw City, where we decided to take a ferry to Mackinac Island. Mackinaw and Mackinac are English and French spellings of the same word, which explains, sort of, why they are both pronounced Mackinaw. (Actually, I recall from high school that there are French words ending in hard "c," so why wouldn't Mackinac be pronounced MackinacK? Hmm? I don't know either.)

Our campmates with the two little boys had told us to be sure to have lunch at Mama Mia's. Mackinaw City is a tourist town, and Mama Mia's pizzeria was touristy, but the pizza was not bad. Besides, the place had a museum in it that detailed the history of the building of the Mackinaw Bridge that connected the lower and upper peninsulas of Michigan. The museum was sort of closed for renovation, but you could walk through it anyway.

We caught a ferry over to Mackinac Island—no cars allowed, and the horses that pulled the carriages were still there and would be for a few more weeks until they were taken off the island for the winter. We wandered up and down the main street and talked to a very nice woman in a tourist booth about accommodations. Not a problem this time of year, she told us as she gave us a list, and things have been a little slower than usual anyway (the economy again). We walked over to the Bayview B&B. Our lodgings price sheet suggested it might be a little steep, and the greeting from one of the two ladies behind the counter was a little cool, so we were not optimistic (in fairness, we did look a bit like hobos, soggy ones at that, who could easily sully the reputation of this refined establishment). The other woman was much more cordial, however, and suggested that as we were walk-ins she could knock the price down a bit—actually quite a bit from $125 to $95. I didn't understand why disreputable looking walk-ins were entitled to this special consideration, but kept my quandary to myself. Perhaps we reminded her of a kindly old uncle back home. A let down, not unlike the first time I was called "sir" in a singles bar and realized that my advancing years (I was 30) were discernible even in a dimly lit pub.

We settled in our room right inside the front door and then headed back out into the rain to explore, our ultimate destination being the very grand Grand Hotel at the top of the hill, a relic of the golden age when presidents and the rich folks from Detroit came up for the summer to escape the heat. We wanted to have drinks on the long porch—some 660 feet long and said to be the longest in the world—that looked out over the juncture of Lake Huron and Lake Michigan, but the wet weather drove us into the cupola bar at the top of the hotel. We had to stop at the tourist desk and pay a $12 admission fee to a charming and quite flirtatious young woman from Bulgaria named Ralitsa. She had just finished explaining the entrance rules to a string of elderly couples and looked bored, but brightened considerably when we walked up. She was positively effusive, which I attributed to my apparent charm and its effect on women 40 years my junior. Wade ungraciously insisted that there was certainly another explanation, perhaps involving a resemblance to a kindly old uncle back home in Bulgaria.

We encountered very few Americans working in the tourist haunts here. The candy shops (every other store on the main street sells fudge) were run by young Eastern Europeans. Whatever happened to the eager young local kids who looked forward to a summer counseling kids at camp, or strutting around the pool as lifeguards, or selling candy and frozen custard at a summer resort? There are still eager kids around, I guess; just imported from Bulgaria.

The barmen at the Grand were all Jamaican—there were a lot of Jamaicans in town doing all kinds of hotel work. Our waiter let us know in a soft whisper that even though the Grand Hotel's policy was "no tips" he would be happy to accept one. We demurred.

There were flags at half-mast everywhere and we could not understand why...until we remembered it was 9/11. Time slips away when you are on the road. It felt good, though, to be in a part of the world where people still liked Americans. There weren't that many such places left, and here we were so conveniently close to home.

A so-so dinner at the Astor St. Cafe, cute little place with a wall mural of Mackinac done in primitive style. The waitress and the cook were both American, which was a selling point of sorts. I gave the whitefish a try. Why is it that so many waterside resorts make such disappointing fish? I made a note that the cafe is somehow associated with Ernest Hemingway, who spent his summers in Michigan and his honeymoon on Mackinac.

Back to the Bayview for a chat with a couple who had lived in Washington, DC, where I spent my early childhood and a fair amount of my early adulthood, too. They had gone to a state fair and seen a llama. She said she wanted one, and to oblige her her husband bought her one. They now have a llama farm with 56 of the things. They didn't get away much because of the animals, but decided to take a few days off and come up to Mackinac. Their 30th or 40th anniversary, I think.

One of the fun things about road trips is the people you get to talk to. I maintain that everyone has an interesting life story to tell. Sometimes it isn't told very well, but it is almost always told by a person who thinks it's pretty fascinating, and he or she is often right. I am quick to ask questions to tease out more details, and those details are readily forthcoming. People are eager to talk about themselves, but frequently far less curious about others. I am accustomed to asking the questions and having few if any asked about me. Fortunately, I'm a very good listener.

We moved inside for evening dessert, a tradition at the place, and had strawberry shortcake. We retired to our room to watch the congressional hearings on Iraq with Crocker and Petraeus—very impressive.

September 12—The Upper Peninsula of Michigan

Both of us had brought along books to read. I had decided to begin by re-reading Kerouac's *On the Road*, which I had not looked at since I was in college 40 years ago. It also happened to be the 50th anniversary of its publication, so there was a lot of hooha about it in the press. It had been a bit of a struggle for me the first time. Not that the prose was all that elusive, but I had been a tightass college sophomore, pretty conservative, and just found most of it amoral and distasteful. I had lived a lot since then. Perhaps this read would be different.

I would also re-read *Blue Highways*, the real inspiration for our trip. Seemed to me there were more episodes when I read it the first time, but I think I had added a few mentally from other sources over the years. All in all, it held up well, and the richness of Moon's encounters with just plain folks set the bar for us, one that was beyond our reach most of the time, but gave us something to shoot for all the same.

Wade was working on C.S. Lewis' *Surprised by Joy*, a book that had been recommended by fellow members of a men's Christian study group. Wade had become intensely interested in religion and was wrestling with whether he should join a church that many of his friends and neighbors—not to mention his wife—had already adopted. I have noticed that many of my friends and relatives became more spiritual as they got older. More time to think surely is one reason. A more seasoned worldview perhaps another. Then there is a possible sense that so much of life's important work—career, family, etc.—lay behind them. Maybe this stage of life is the time to place it all in a larger, universal context. Theological introspection was not part of my journey—I had been there some years ago, and my partner is an Episcopal priest. It was high on Wade's agenda, however, and I was happy to be a sounding board and for the stimulating conversations that ensued.

So, here we were: two men in our 60s who had seen much of the world (50+ countries for me in numerous travels and 6 or so years living overseas, and every state in the union; Wade is a Vietnam vet, had lived in a half dozen states I guess and seen a good bit of the Far East and Europe). We had both lived well and had had many interesting jobs. We were both reasonably gregarious, with many people we would call good friends. And, while I did not have a wife (of 36 years) and a son as Wade did, I had been in a committed relationship for over 30 years and had taken many young people under my wing during that time, many of whom now had families of their own with whom I had remained close.

But now what? What to make of the six decades that had gone before, and, more importantly, what of the two more or less that still lay before us? This self-scrutinizing voyage was a chance to step back, to examine some unfamiliar lives that we would encounter along the way, and for each of us to try out some theories of our own life on another person we knew well, whose intellect we respected, and who could be counted on for an honest and thoughtful reaction. In sum, a very worthwhile reality check while life still afforded us the time to act on it.

We had agreed that each of us would keep a journal of the trip and compare our recollections at the end, at least those that we felt like sharing. As it had occurred to me early on, on Ocracoke, actually, after some preliminary discussions with Wade about religion, this trip was not just about seeing new sights and meeting new people, though there would certainly be much of that. It was to be as much a journey of self-discovery (not to coin a phrase), and a journal was the perfect tool for collecting one's thoughts and charting the change in one's perspective during the trip.

But a major part of the process was enjoying each day as it came. The next morning the Bayview treated us to peach French toast for breakfast—certainly the best breakfast, if not the best meal, we were to have on the entire trip. Once again we were served by a Jamaican dining room staff, this time to the accompaniment of Jamaican music.

We took the ferry back to Mackinaw City and then headed north over the Mackinaw Bridge (the Mighty Mac) to the Upper Peninsula, land of the "yoopers." We decided to head along Route 2 that hugs the southern coast of the peninsula along Lake Michigan. Not a lot of people or traffic and more than a few abandoned—or nearly so—resorts. You could tell that the economy had not been any kinder to the upper part of the state than it had to the lower.

Outside a small roadside store there was a sign for smoked fish. We decided to give it another chance. The little shop had a world map with pins to mark where you were from, so we poked holes in Northeastern Pennsylvania and the Tidewater Virginia area, squeezing them among the hundreds pressed in by those who had come before. We were the only customers, so the proprietor had time to talk. He showed us his assortment of smoked fish...and it was an assortment this time, several different types...this was more like it. I bought another round, but from the expression on Wade's face it was clear that this was a treat I would enjoy entirely on my own.

In Manistique we stopped to take pictures of an historic old brick water tower, the lower part of which had been turned into a local museum that was, unfortunately, closed. As we marveled at the place, a middle-aged man walked by and told us his father had helped build the tower. We thought he could give us some more information on the structure—he couldn't. "Don't really know much about it," he said. "Have a good day." Though historic preservation is pretty widespread, this was further evidence to me that the fascination with it often doesn't run very deep.

On to Minisung and lunch at the Dogpatch Cafe, an establishment replete with wall paintings of L'il Abner, Daisy Mae, and the whole Yokum Clan. It had been there since 1966, when Al Capp's strip about life in the hollers was still popular (before his unfortunate co-ed incident—a harbinger of the sexual harassment frenzy that would come twenty years later and would subside only when it inculpated the nation's chief executive thirty years later). I always loved the comic strip, and his troubles did not seem to dim his memory here.

Continuing west we passed a sign that advertised 40,000 hubcaps and wheelcovers. I believed it; the hillside was buried under a mass of disks glittering in the sun. And as I happened to be one short on my '93 Nissan Sentra back home, I insisted we stop and take a chance. Craig Tasson ran the place part-time for his dad, James, who toodled over in his wheelchair to see what was going on (a camper with out-of-state plates and a couple of ratty looking would-be tourists —no wonder his suspicions were aroused). Anyway, they had ONE wheelcover for a '93 Nissan Sentra. And, Craig knew just where, amidst all of the other 39,999 spread over the lot, to find it. He disappeared into the sea of chrome and stainless steel and returned with exactly the right one a few minutes later. I was amazed, and said so.

We pulled up to Van Riper State Park (site #111 at $21 a night Wade reminds me). Two late-teenage girls at the office seemed pretty happy to see us and wanted to make sure that we were going to be there over the weekend for the annual Harvest Fest. They seemed especially earnest—my charm at work again, I was sure. Wade was equally certain of his opposite opinion. In any case, when we informed them that we had a train to catch and would be moving on they seemed sincerely disappointed.

September 13—Lake Superior

It was bright and sunny when we set out to continue on our way across the southern Lake Michigan coast of the Upper Peninsula. We cut north across the peninsula toward Lake Superior to Baraga, a place about which we knew absolutely nothing. We saw a sign for The Shrine of the Snowshoe Priest, which was kind of tantalizing, so we followed a side road down to a large statue of a priest holding a cross. Six stories tall, the priest held a 7-foot cross and had 26-foot snowshoes. The odd part was that he was suspended on a platform that had four curved iron legs that were shrouded at the bottom in white. It looked a bit like he was standing on a large four-legged spider with tepees for slippers.

A Slovenian by birth, Baraga (for whom the town is named) came to the United States in 1830 to what was then the Diocese of Cincinnati and was sent off to minister to the Indians of Michigan. He traveled hundreds of miles during the winters on snowshoes, hence the name (kind of diminishes the momentousness of traversing the same territory by turning an ignition key and cruising in air-conditioned comfort). He learned the Ottawa and Ojibway (Anglicized as Chippewa) languages, mastering Ojibway so well that he published a dictionary that is still used today. He eventually became bishop of his own diocese (Diocese of Marquette). I made a note to read up on him when I got back home.

There was a gift shop/snack bar with a sign advertising that it (but not the rest of the building) was for sale. A very nice woman had been running it for some time and was ready to retire. She looked hopeful when we inquired about it, then crestfallen when she found we were merely curious and just passing through.

On our way west and north we stopped in the Ojibwa Casino to see if there were any local festivals we should know about (there weren't). One of the ideas we had had was to stop in at local fests, church dinners, etc., and just get to meet the local folks. Seems, however, that we were too late for the summer events and too early for the holiday ones. We passed through town after town with no luck. The real disappointment was missing out on the home-cooked food that is often available at dirt cheap prices in church parish halls. Events like that saw me healthily through college.

Wade was not much interested in casinos, but I like to hear the kaching of the slots. After 10 minutes or so, however, it was clear he had lost what miniscule interest he had in the first place, so I cashed in a dollar ahead and we pressed on. I was certain there would be more casinos along the way (there were), as it is getting harder and harder to find places that don't have them. I recall when Atlantic City opened its first gambling palace and how excited everyone, including me, had been to experience the place. Though I still find these establishments interesting from time to time, the luster has most certainly worn off. Actually kind of sad to see how many people live their lives in them, and how dependent we have become as a society on vices (I include smoking here) as revenue sources to finance our schools and public services. Somewhere along the way, with the further stimulus of unrestrained borrowing, we have lost the will or ability to make economic choices.

Skies were turning pretty dark when we arrived in Houghton, a nice college town—home of Michigan Tech. We lunched in an old library that had been turned into a brew pub restaurant.

We decided to head up a little finger of land sticking out into Lake Superior called the Keweenaw Peninsula, all the way to Copper Harbor, the last town on U.S. 41 that stretches all the way down to Florida. We camped for the night at Fort Wilkins State Park (site #165, 23 bucks). The RV next to us was from the very Virginia peninsula that Wade hails from... small world. We were to spend most nights in a state or provincial park (sometimes a municipal one), several times catching them the last day before they closed for the season. I wondered how much money we saved taking a camper and staying in parks for less than $40 a night. Not much when you figure in the gas, I suppose, but that wasn't the point. Wade said more than once that sitting outside under the stars was something he really enjoyed. No TV, and, at this time of year, not much in the way of other campers. Very peaceful and a good arrangement for two old friends who were trying to decode the mysteries of life together.

We staked out our site and headed back into Copper Harbor, looking for some kind of tourist information office. We saw an information sign attached to George and Brenda's Jam and Ice Cream shop. The shop was actually closed, but we could see George and Brenda inside so we went in anyway. They were making apple butter and were happy to chat about the history of the area, which they had observed for 60 years. Apparently the local folks had mined copper until the lumps of the metal became too big to manage. Wade and I talked about this afterward and had a little trouble making sense of it, what with all the building sites being raided for copper wire. The price of the stuff would have seemed to make a place with piano-sized chunks of copper a virtual gold mine (sorry).

George also told us about their jam business and the difference between blueberries, huckleberries and bilberries. They are similar but diminish in sweetness in that order. He also said that the berry season was off by 75% because of lack of snowfall and rain.

Before we turned in we went up to the Keweenaw Mountain Lodge, built in 1934 as a project of the Civil Works Administration during the Depression. Nice stone and woodwork, but we decided not to stick around for dinner and headed back to camp.

September 14—Wisconsin

We had breakfast in Copper Harbor. Our waitress for a day, Claudette, was in town helping her friend who owned the place. There was a small party at a table near the front—a going-away party from the looks of it. A family was saying goodbye to two European girls who were leaving after working the summer in Copper Harbor. A heartwarming picture, obviously more than simple mutual respect and thankfulness. You could sense that the American family had grown by two during the past few months. A happy cultural exchange, but it made me wonder how many American kids were spending their summers working in Eastern Europe.

From Copper Harbor we drove right along the shore of Lake Superior in a strong wind that chopped the water so that it looked like the Atlantic Ocean. Watching the whitecaps, you could appreciate the forces that swallowed the Edmund Fitzgerald.

We got into Ironwood, Michigan, late morning and wandered around looking for a good place for lunch. We parked and walked along the sidewalk scouting prospects, then asked a couple of middle-aged guys for a recommendation. Paul A. Sturgul (his card read) and his friend Brian told us to follow them to the Pines—best place in town, they said. Turned out that Paul was a friend of a friend of Wade's (Jim Bill, a William & Mary professor) in Williamsburg, so he and

Wade had something to talk about. Good recommendation on the restaurant—I had a chocolate shake that was good enough to remind me what I had been missing over the years. They are back on my list of regulars.

Shortly after lunch we crossed into Wisconsin and headed up to Bayfield, where we had heard about the Scarecrow Festival. There were some scarecrows about, but not enough to tempt us to hang around for the festival, so we proceeded on to Duluth. On the other side of town we stopped for gas. A very engaging young pump attendant, a senior in high school, was eager to talk to strangers and bounce ideas about his future off on us. He was taking computer automated design courses and wanted to make cars his career. We talked about Nascar, mechanics school, and his 1988 Trans Am, of which he was extremely proud. He wasn't sure he was doing the right thing (who could be at his age), but we opined that if cars were his passion—and they obviously were—he was probably on the right track. He also had enough charm and enthusiasm to do well no matter what. Funny how young men can be so exuberant around strangers and so taciturn with their own families. I can recall many occasions when my father would question me about what I was up to and got monosyllables in response. Then when a friend's dad would show an interest in me, I would babble away.

I paid for the gas and waved goodbye to the future of America, feeling reassured about its promise and vitality after this brief exchange. Wade and I had discussed several ways of splitting the cost of the trip. Neither of us enthuses over itemizing expenses—more of a guy thing I have come to find—though he is very methodical about keeping a log of gas and mileage. So, we agreed that I would buy the gas and breakfast and he would buy the groceries, the occasional dinner out, and pay the campsite fees. Extraordinary costs, like train fare and the B&Bs we stayed at a couple of nights, we just split. It was a fair arrangement notwithstanding the price of gas that inched up daily as we traveled, and soared when we crossed the Canadian border.

Dinner in Eveleth, Minnesota, at a roadhouse called Timbers. They had a girl in a booth selling some kind of instant gambling tickets, which I have a hard time resisting. I bought some for Wade and me...and we both lost.

We wrapped up what Wade called the "longest day behind the wheel" (12 hours over three states) and headed out Route 58 to spend the night at a place called Veterans Campsite, site #14 @ $18. It was 9 p.m. and we both dropped off to sleep as soon as we got under the covers.

September 15—On to Canada

We drove back into Eveleth for breakfast, past a giant hockey stick that advertised a place called the Hippodrome. Eveleth is a pretty depressed place—those establishments on the main street that weren't boarded up were mostly either bars or liquor stores. If there was a good place for breakfast, we missed it. We drove on to Virginia and had donuts at a bakery on Main St., where our ribbing of each other amused the waitresses. There was only one other customer and no movement on the street, so as far as entertainment went, we were it.

Next stop was a gas-up in Orr, Minnesota. While I filled the tank, Wade wandered into the garage and struck up a conversation with a man who had worked at Newport News Shipyard from 1946 to 1950. He reminisced about ship construction techniques, and Wade compared them to what he remembered about building submarines and aircraft carriers from his days at Newport News twenty years later. The man was now living in New Mexico and was out visiting his son and daughter-in-law and doing some fishing. His wife had died, and he shared that his life was disjointed and unattached. I suspect this is one reason why widowers remarry more often than widows (though the sex ratio no doubt is a significant factor). Old men whose lives were their work, and who consigned so much of their social lives to their spouses, easily become disconnected when both their careers and their better halves are gone. Finding a new better half quick is one solution.

The plan was for us to lunch in International Falls, then cross the border into Canada. I had heard so much about the town—it always seems to be on TV as the coldest place in the U.S. during the winter. As much publicity as it gets, I assumed it must be a pretty hopping place. But…no. Not much in the way of eateries either. We were lured into what from the outside looked like a kind of trattoria, but once inside discovered that it was a rather noisy gaming arcade that served pizza.

So far on this trip, we had had very few "aha" gastronomical moments. There was the French Laundry in Fenton and a couple of good breakfasts; I have already commented on the peach French toast in Mackinac. On the whole, however, there were very few restaurants that I would care to recommend to the hungry traveler who might choose to follow in our footsteps. That was a surprise to someone from the New York metro area who is used to good food as the normal course of things in whatever establishment one might duck into. Beyond that, in many years of traveling for business and pleasure, I have prided myself on being able to pick out the real diamond in the rough from the rock pile of roadside beaneries. More than once on this trip, however, I was seduced by the promise of something akin to Mom's home cooking, only to find it was more reminiscent of one of my old mess hall sergeant's off days. We learned to keep muffins and fruit around for breakfast and snacks, and cooked our own simple dinners at the camper at least half the time. The good news was that my pants were feeling a bit loose. Addicted to good food—especially desserts, especially ice cream— as I am, the temporary lack of culinary enticement was a good thing: a chance to shape up and slim down before returning to the glorious land of Gastronomia.

We crossed the American border, passing the Boise Cascade plant that was on the river where the falls of International Falls used to be. The American border folks were pleasant enough. Not so the Canadians, who decided that two old guys in a camper were about as suspicious a gang as had attempted to penetrate the perimeter of their homeland in many a moon. They insisted on taking the camper apart while we were told to watch from a distance. They asked lots of questions about what we did for a living. As neither of us was all that busy at the moment—worse yet, I claimed to be a writer (what was I thinking?)—they redoubled their efforts to find the real source of our income secreted in some hidden camper compartment. They came away frustrated and decidedly unhappy, probably convinced that the "stuff" was there someplace and that we had put one over on them. Fortunately for us, a caravan of nuns of some sort (women with headscarves in some minivans) came through at that moment. The border guards brightened right up, rousted them out of their vehicles and plunged into the bowels of their backseats. We were yesterday's news.

A few feet further on was the Ontario welcome center. An attractive but not particularly well-informed young woman had very little in the way of useful information to pass along. We were actually better informed in the local attractions department. We told her about a local "fiesta" that we had seen advertised. She thanked us for the tip and said she and her boyfriend would make a point of taking it in that weekend. "You're welcome" we said cheerily with just the slightest hint of sarcasm and headed off to Rushing River Provincial Park just south of Kenora, where we stopped for two nights to give us a chance to catch up on our reading and dirty laundry, in that order.

September 16—Rushing River, Ontario

The drive from International Falls to Kenora along the Lake of the Woods was one of the high points of the trip. Straight roads, lots of water and trees with very few houses, and a terrain that varies less than 100 feet—probably much like coastal New England of 400 years ago. Wade said that he felt challenged in the same way as he had on his Alaska trip—how does one "can" these times and feelings for the "dry" times? Possible solutions: take more pictures and write down one's impressions as close to real time as possible. We agreed to keep our personal journals with that in mind.

Sunday was a day of rest and relaxation. It was the last day the Rushing River Provincial Park (site #36 at 30$C/night) would be open, and it was bright, warm and sunny, so we decided to sit in the sun and read. We had expected colder temperatures and had brought the right clothes for it, but so far the days had been surprisingly warm. Wade and I each picked out nice sunny spots near the lake to read. Wade took breaks to take walks and check out the waterfall. He had brought two bikes along with the hope that he might induce me to change my mind about two-wheelers and join him in a pedaling side trip. No way. I had grown up with bikes as my only transport and had spent too many hours fighting the hills and the wind. As bike technology developed, and as I got older and wider, the bikes seemed to have become increasingly uncomfortable. Skinny little seats, handlebars down by your knees—these advances just added to the discomfort I recalled all too well from my childhood. And most serious bikers I know have been knocked off their vehicles by errant motorists at least once, so the heightened need for vigilance and looking over one's shoulder further diminished the two-wheeled experience for me. On those occasions when Wade could no longer fight the lure of the wide-open and exposed road, he savored it by himself.

It was clear and around 70 degrees. Several days earlier they had 12" of snow. Further south we had run into sleet in Ironwood, Michigan, about the same time. But today the warm sun made it a perfect time to kick back. Wade spent the early afternoon sitting on a rock looking at Dogtooth Lake. He said he was trying to picture a desert nomad in this situation; all this water going by without any signs of real civilization save for a foot bridge made of steel and a roadway bridge of wood.

We talked about raising children and why some turned out well and others did not. Wade concluded that there was a formula (he has little faith in luck). Examining those families that are significantly more successful with producing adults who are financially and emotionally independent, he says, a couple of things stand out:

1. raising good kids as a priority works
2. smarter parents have a better chance to produce a happy young adult
3. the number of kids in the family doesn't seem to matter
4. a strong family unit is essential for a lifestyle to survive
5. a proactive education process improves the odds

It was never clearly established exactly what was meant by "smart." Certainly I have known a lot of people who were skill smart who had messy unhappy lives, and others with emotional smarts that did not translate into financial success or renown within their careers. I think that much of what we regard as success is more a function of ambition than intelligence. I also believe that unexpected events— you can't anticipate everything—often get in the way. In the days of the military draft, no matter how bright, well-intentioned, or focused a father was, the fact that he wasn't around (a factor beyond his control) limited his positive influence. Even more drastic if he didn't come back.

I granted Wade that much of what he posited sounded reasonable, but that for some reason or other good kids came from bad families and bad kids came from good ones. Arguably, however, the stats were in his favor.

Today I would finish Kerouac's classic *On the Road*. As I said, I had read it 40 some years earlier while I was an undergraduate in college. "Beat" was still in then. Maynard G. Krebs was chumming around with his preppy friend Dobie Gillis on TV, and the stereotypical goateed bongo drummer popped up all over pop culture. Jack Kerouac and his book were supposedly the genesis of it all, though he was somewhat uncomfortable with the attribution. Nevertheless, the lure of Route 66 proved irresistible for his disciples—many of whom I suspect had never actually read the book.

My memories of it were fuzzy. I recalled a couple of guys tooling back and forth across the country, but other than that it had affected me far less at the time than *Atlas Shrugged* and *The Hobbit*. Anyway, this time around there was nothing quite so unsettling about Kerouac's cast of characters. They seemed kind of sad. I was able to appreciate his skill with words, though, in a way that would not have been possible back in the 60s. No question the man was a writer. Some passages were so well crafted I read them several times just to soak in their pure poetry. I could also understand how his romantic portrait of two footloose guys with no responsibilities whatsoever and little to occupy their time but partying, amusing themselves with a gaggle of willing young women, and of course driving, would stimulate the fantasies of the adolescent that resides within many of us—within me anyway. Still, it was a period piece. The search for "it" and "knowing time" and the callous unconcern for the sensitivities of others seemed pretty dated. It was also a window on a simpler time when the cavorting of Sal Paradise and Dean Moriarty and their compatriots could shock the reader. No more. The world has raced past them.

The sanitized version, the TV series *Route 66*, was more my speed (slower) and stoked my imagination about the joys of the open road. It had also been the source of my first choice in destinations, and I still hope to do old Route 66 in a convertible some day.

I finished that book, then picked up *Blue Highways*, the book that had stimulated me the way *On the Road* had done to men of an earlier generation. Re-reading it after 25 years was an entirely different experience from that of the book I had just put down. It was wonderful. As gripping to me as the first time, and Moon's way with words made each paragraph (not just the selected passage as with Kerouac) pure joy. I may have to read it yet again when I am through.

Wade wants to do a CD of the trip, a composite of the pictures he and I take with our digital cameras. "Okay" I said. Okay was not good enough. If there is an adjective to describe my traveling buddy, it is "exuberant." He approaches pretty much every activity with unrestrained enthusiasm. Or, he doesn't approach it at all. If he's not excited about it, he just doesn't do it. I envy that in a way. Much of my life, and I suspect just about everyone else's, is made up of a handful of undertakings we detest, another handful that stir our passions, and a whole lot of in between. I ratcheted my response up a notch. "I think we really should do it." I sort of gushed. Not quite as much as he was hoping for, but he accepted it.

I had bought a digital camera 5 years earlier, and it seemed to work for a while, but it had recently developed the unsettling habit of failing to perform out of doors. Inside shots mostly came out okay, mostly, but any attempts at sunlight shooting and the camera just shut off. That just wouldn't do for what would essentially be a month in the country.

So, a few weeks before we set sail I went down to the local Radio Shack and picked up a new one on special. I read the manual as carefully as I could, which didn't take long. After several pages of warnings (like, do not hold the unit underwater for long periods of time) there were a few more pages of graphics that named the various buttons, a short how-to on getting the thing up and running, and a sequence of the buttons to press to take a picture. There were also a half dozen trouble-shooting hints in the unlikely event any of the stock situations occurred (none of them did—all my problems had apparently not been anticipated by the creators of the slim little manual). That was it! At the halfway point in the manual there were still more pages, but turning the book around and reading the same information in Spanish left me no better informed than I had been in the first place.

After taking a dozen pictures a message appeared telling me the camera was full. I was incredulous. Fortunately, the clerk at Radio Shack had insisted I buy a spare memory card. When I went to insert it, I found that it was not a spare—it was my only memory card—and that it was the limited memory built in to the camera itself that was full. That problem solved, I immediately detected a new one. I could only take pictures in black and white. So much for vivid landscapes. Eventually I would figure out the proper settings, but only after some great photo-ops had slipped by.

That night over dinner at a local Chinese restaurant, Wade and I talked about my original idea for a cross-country tour, and the 1961 Yellow Chevy Impala convertible that I had wanted to take the tour in. Wade has restored some cars himself and considers such endeavors child's play. Literally, as a matter of fact—he bought an old Ford Mustang to restore with his son Will. Producing a finished classic was secondary. The primary motive was to come up with a project he and Will could work on together that would encourage the boy to spend more time at home—the prospect of a cool car of his own was the carrot. Clever. My respect for his insights on child-rearing grew.

Anyhow, Wade believes that anyone has the instincts to master the craft and that I would be a better person for having restored my own antique. The jury is out on this, and the case could drag on a lifetime, but it did set me to thinking.

September 17—Manitoba

We set out early for Winnipeg, stopping for breakfast in the nearby resort town of Kenora, Ontario, a major (the major?) resort town on the Lake of the Woods. It was originally named Rat Portage—a reference to the fur industry when the area was on the way to some good places to trap muskrat. As the area developed it became a center for, among other things, flour. Having a name like Rat Portage on your bags of flour was bad for business, so at the beginning of the last century businesses pushed for a name change. They took the first two letters of two nearby towns, Keewatin and Norman, and added the first two of the original name (Rat, remember?) and came up with Kenora.

Our choice for breakfast was a small restaurant in a downtown hotel that had recently suffered a fire, clearing out most of the paying customers for a while. Too bad for the restaurant proprietor, Linda, an engaging woman who had been talked into investing in the restaurant by her son, who decided a month or two into the venture that he needed a regular job to support his kids and left his mother to go it alone. She was upbeat, though, bless her, and thought it was a good change from her former profession as school bus driver. That was an opening to start in again on the subject of raising, and civilizing, children. We had a good chat about schools and discipline and the merits of holding kids back, which the three of us agreed wasn't always such a bad thing, self-esteem issues notwithstanding. As I said, business was pretty slow so Linda had plenty of time to talk.

After breakfast, we headed off toward Winnipeg on a very flat and straight stretch of the trans-Canada highway, stopping to take pictures of each other at the big Welcome to Manitoba sign. There was a large billboard for a Mennonite Village that made it look like a good place to stop. We had been light on tourist attractions and local festivals so far, so we both felt we had some catching up to do. Unhappily, we saw no more signs for the village, and we both were keeping a watchful eye, but must have shot right past it.

We circled north of Winnipeg and took Route 6 up to Warren. A woman at a local gas station said how much she envied us for going to Churchill to see polar bears. She was not the first, nor would she be the last, to tell us this. And it didn't seem to matter how close to Churchill we got, we still encountered people every day who "had always wanted to go to Churchill." Her son lived in Gillam, the last stop on the road north, after which you have to train it. He made the north–south drive frequently, and he *had* been to Churchill. His accounts of the place fueled her interest, but apparently not enough to stir her to action.

Lunch was at a place next door called the Trails Café where a friendly waitress (after leaving the border police behind, everyone we ran into was friendly) filled us in on the First Nations. These are sort of equivalent to our Indian reservations and have some degree of self-government, including their own police forces, though there seems to be some variation among the 600 or so First Nation reserves. We were to wander in and out of a number of these enclaves during the trip, mostly in Ontario.

I got behind the wheel for the first time. I am a cheerful passenger provided the driver is capable, and Wade drives well. And, although I will happily drive my own vehicles from one end of the country to the other, I do not leap at the chance to drive other people's cars. Still, it was clearly my turn, and Wade, willing chauffeur though he'd been, was ready for a break.

Religion came up again. Wade had wanted to have a serious talk with my partner Charles, an ordained Episcopal minister of 40-odd years, but found Charles too busy for the kind of at-length dialogue Wade was looking for. I assured him that this would not always be the case and that the colloquy he sought lay ahead in the not too distant future.

Eighty miles north of Warren there was a noticeable decrease in the number of pines and firs. There were now more low scrubs with some ash. The road rested on a 6-foot berm to prevent frost heave.

I drove on, becoming more aware that as the population became thinner, gas stations became rarer. The camper got 13 to 14 miles to the gallon, not too bad because it had a 6-cylinder engine. Its gas tank was small, however, so it needed to stop for a drink every couple hundred miles. I was buying the gas, and it took me a little while to grow accustomed to prices quoted in litres. And to prices that were about double what we paid in the States.

A quick stop for gas in Saint Martin's and then up to Grand Rapids. Wade had picked out a place called Moak Lodge on the Internet, so we asked directions and headed down a long dirt road that "T"ed at a lake. We turned right and found the place, but there was a barrier across the road. I could hear voices on the other side, so I crawled under the barrier and walked over to a camper where there was a family cookout going on. "Yes, we're closed," they said. "What's the next best place," we asked. Grins all around. There apparently was no next best place really, but they finally conceded there might be a least worst. We were tired and it was getting dark and the weather wasn't good, so that would have to do.

We drove back to the sign for Hobbs campground and took the short drive down to some campsites on the lake, where we could find no one in charge. A fisherman from Minnesota was just pulling in with what we thought was a respectable catch—he said it was lousy and blamed it on the weather. He came up every year with his wife and mother in law, both of whom emerged from a nearby cabin. They seemed to get along okay, but the mother in law appeared to be calling the shots. They gathered up the fish and headed back to the cabin. Grab a spot, the man told us, and someone would be around in the morning

That night as we listened to the waves lapping a few feet from our camper, Wade and I had a long talk about changes in water levels around the world. I related a theory I had heard that a sudden rise in sea levels worldwide might be one possible explanation for the great flood stories that seem to be part of so many cultural histories, even as far away as aboriginal Australia. The idea is that rather than a gradual rise following the last ice age, there had been a sudden surge that inundated coastal cities all over the place, perhaps as the result of the failure of an ice dam somewhere. Wade had doubts about surges of water big enough to cause that kind of rise. I then suggested that ancient Lake Missoula, which may have been as much as 2000 feet deep and contained more water than the Great Lakes had reportedly flooded the west several times when its ice dams broke and that similar events have occurred elsewhere in the world.

I recommended a book I had read that posited just this concept: *Underworld, The Mysterious Origins of Civilization* by Graham Hancock. Hancock described cities under the ocean in various parts of the world that he was busily discovering to prove his point. His idea is that a lot of these coastal cities in places like India and Japan were swamped by a sudden rise in ocean levels of 100 meters somewhere between 7000 and 17000 years ago. Folks living safely inland incorporated tales of the catastrophe into their histories and passed them down from one generation to the next where they remained as part of an oral tradition, or with luck a written one such as Genesis or Gilgamesh. Hancock has been dismissed by some as a crackpot, but it seems that the idea of one or more dramatic surges in sea level is gaining some currency. I promised to lend Wade the book.

1. Wade sets up camp at Ocracoke, North Carolina in April

2. Getting off the ferry at Mackinac Island, Michigan

3. Mackinac Island – The Bayview B&B

4. Statue of the Snowshoe Priest, Baraga, Michigan

5. *Camping at Lake of the Woods, Ontario*

6. *The Rotary Bridge, Pisew Falls, Manitoba*

7. Perplexed engineer being rescued by Canada Automobile Association after running out of gas.

8. John catches up on his reading after dinner.

9. Boarding the train for Churchill – Thompson, Manitoba

10. *One of Churchill's many inukshuks.*

11. A polar bear trap, Churchill, Manitoba

12. *Tundra buggies in Churchill, Manitoba*

13. One of the many warning signs that surround Churchill

14. Churchill – picture of a polar bear, taken from a safe distance.

15 Churchill – Close-up of John posing in front of fake polar bear with hometown newspaper.

16. Ile De Bellevue, Saskatchewan – The monument to the brown pea

17. Wade photographs a group of students and guide in Batoche, Saskatchewan

18. Moose Jaw, Saskatchewan – Mac the Moose under reconstruction.

19. John and Wade with Charlie Vesely in Amana, Iowa

20. With a team of oxen in Nauvoo, Illinois

21. Rebuilt Mormon temple, Nauvoo, Illinois.

September 18—Thompson

The weather was dark and windy when Wade hit the road for Thompson, our northernmost driving destination. From there we would take the train up to Churchill. Halfway there we pulled into an outpost called Trees in a town—or maybe a dot on the map—called Ponton. From the road we thought the place was closed, but it turned out to be a nice motel/store/restaurant that was very much open for business. The crew there worked two-week shifts and then headed south for two weeks. Our waitress had been bussing back and forth from Winnipeg for a couple of years.

We reached Thompson by late afternoon. It's a modern town of about 16,000 people that has two McDonald's and a Wal-Mart. We had not bought our train tickets yet and were still toying with the idea of driving to Gillam, a midpoint between Thompson and Churchill a couple of hundred miles up a dirt road. From there we would have no choice but to train it, as there was no road of any kind beyond that.

Stopping in at the local Heritage Museum and tourist information office, we met a charmer named Tanna Heintz whom we asked for advice. She counseled us against driving up to Gillam. It was a bone-jarring dirt road from Thompson, she said, and there was really no secure place to park once we got there. What about the freight train, we asked. We had heard that the freight had one car at the end reserved for passengers and that it made the trip in the daytime instead of at night as the regular passenger train did. She hadn't heard anything about a freight train, and she should know. She also told us that any concerns we had about the availability of tickets for the passenger train we could dismiss. We had missed Churchill's Beluga whale season, and we were several weeks early for the polar bear season, so there was a lull in tourists and getting a seat should be no problem.

We decided to catch the train that left on Thursday the 19th and to come back on the one that returned on Sunday the 23rd. Officially, the train took 14 hours. Actual time was a different matter all together, sometimes 24 hours or more. There were stories of tourists who planned to spend a day in Churchill, booking the night train up and the next night's return train back. Unfortunately, as the trains were notoriously late, these luckless travelers often arrived in Churchill with only enough time for a quick bite to eat before they had to catch the train back to Thompson. No polar bears for them.

Tanna recommended the Riverfront Café in Thompson, a place next to the float plane terminal that specialized in Chinese food. We sampled okay Chinese while listening to a trio of two young women and a young man discussing the difficulties in finding a place to pee on the road between Thompson and...wherever. He said he had never had a problem, which brought on very loud rejoinders about female and male anatomy and how the processes for relieving oneself actually differed. As if the rest of the diners didn't know. Courting, if that was what was going on (hanging out I think it's called these days), has changed a lot.

We camped at a place called McCreedy Park (site #22 at $C27/night). The McCreedys no longer owned it, and a new couple had taken over. They were big into snowmobiling, but of course it was a bit early for that. Once again we were surprised at how much warmer it was than we expected.

One of the big selling points of McCreedy was that we could leave our camper there and they would shuttle us back and forth to the train station. Another was the very warm and comfortable bathrooms with hot showers. The hot water was controlled by a coin-operated machine that gave you 10 minutes for a "loony," the Canadian dollar. Even though Wade's camper had a hot shower, it required firing up the gas heater and using a fair amount of water from the limited supply in the camper's tank. The shower compartment itself was a bit cramped, and the stream of water was somewhat anemic relative to what I was used to. Simpler to identify a camping site that had hot forceful showers close at hand.

September 19—Pisew Falls

We had a good bit of time before the train, so Wade decided we should head back south of town and take in Pisew Falls, a local tourist attraction. We had noticed a big sign for Rotary Bridge there, prominently displaying the international Rotary Symbol. Being a Rotarian, I was kind of curious about what that was all about.

What it was all about was a suspension bridge across the river that gave one a dead on view of the river. The falls were not that high as touristy falls go, but they were fairly wide and the water gushed impressively. I walked out on the bridge and had Wade take my picture from several angles that included the big Rotary wheel. My plan was to take it back to my own chapter and show them what the other guys were doing, maybe challenging them to take on more ambitious projects. (Not likely. As with so many service organizations, maintaining membership was a problem and the active membership was graying, though we had had some luck attracting younger recruits of late.)

On the way out to the falls, we realized that we had misjudged the distance from town and maybe should have gassed up first. Nevertheless, Wade thought we had enough gas to do the trick and was unconcerned by the absence of filling stations along the road. On the way back, my buddy, the consummate engineer who planned for everything, ran out of gas. Not to worry, I thought. We had bought some new gas cans the day before for just such an emergency. What we had neglected to do, however, was put gas in them. So, we coasted to the side of the road and called for help.

One of the discussions we had had before we left home regarded cell phones. Wade had said he saw no need to bring his cell on this trip. He had, however, included a cell phone on the comprehensive list of "to-dos and to-brings" he had given me in August. I would have brought it anyway. I had checked it along the way and found that I could not access my voice mail at all from Canada and often could not get a signal (we already knew that it would be useless in Churchill). At this point, however, it worked fine and got us connected to the Canadian Automobile Association in seconds. They promised to send someone out with 5 gallons of gas right away.

It was a nice day, all in all, and my mood was not dampened a bit by the temporary inconvenience. In fact, the appearance of this single error in judgment, this oversight on the part of the otherwise consummately organized skipper of this uplands excursion, gave me a bit of a lift. And we had operas to help pass the time if need be—I hadn't forgotten them this time. Important to preserve the moment first, though…for posterity. I took lots of pictures of our stranded craft, and its captain, from various angles while we waited to be rescued. I suspect they will come in handy some day. The CAA truck pulled up before I was finished, driven by a humorless young man of few words who poured the contents of his gas can into the camper, got Wade to sign his work order, and drove off.

The 30-minute drive back to Thompson passed in silence, the engineer being in no mood to chat. We gassed up and pulled into McCreedy Park, prepared to catch the train that was scheduled to leave at 5:55. Our hosts saw no need to hurry off to the station, however, as all the locals knew that the scheduled departure wasn't going to happen. We actually boarded at 7:40 and headed north. Then south. Then north again. And so on. For some reason, the train switched back and forth in the yard for an hour and a half. Finally, at 9:10 we were on our way.

It was a nice train, clean and relatively new – a service of VIA Rail Canada, the Canadian passenger service. Only about 20 passengers, so Tanna had been right about there being plenty of space. We wandered into the dining car and had a very salty dinner of pot roast with some wine and dessert. Food wasn't great, but the staff was earnest and anxious to please. We shared the dining car with a half dozen other people, including a couple from Iowa, a college professor who was just back from an overseas trek and would be heading for Mexico shortly, and a couple of other men we chatted with briefly. A young woman doctor from Germany was also on board, but she was too shy to chat with any of the men (let's hope she was into gynecology or pediatrics), though she did warm up to the Iowa couple.

After dinner we went back to our seats—plenty of room for everyone to have his own—and snoozed as the train crept its way north in the dark.

September 20—Churchill

The train pulled into Gillam around 3 a.m. A number of locals got on and off, mostly off. One of the new passengers was a man from Ames, Iowa. He has driven the perimeter of Australia and thought nothing of driving the awful road to Gillam from Thompson in a '99 Ford Escort. He parked his car at the Gillam station, but was concerned about its safety. A look out the window suggested he had reason to be concerned. It was a pretty decrepit looking place. A lot of the housing here, as with some other small communities we had seen along the rail line, looked pretty rundown. Not just old, but vandalized—except that there were people still living there behind the plywooded windows.

The trip from Thompson to Churchill is 380 miles. The passenger train moves very slowly and takes to sidings frequently to let the higher priority freight trains go by. While the train is owned by Canada's VIA rail system, the track and the freight trains are owned by a private company. The track is old, originally laid back in the 20s, largely on permafrost. While it was designed for freight, that design did not anticipate the volume of it. Just about everything in Churchill comes in by train or ship, including the houses the Churchillians live in, which are all prefab. The big shipments, however, are grain. Yesterday's paper said that Churchill's port had had a record year for grain shipments, which are shipped to the port on grain trains 80 cars long, each car weighing 200,000 pounds or so. The heavy trains move the rails up, down, and around, so they are inspected every day and the maximum speeds reset section by section accordingly. So, even though the theoretical maximum speed is 30 miles an hour, the train often goes a lot slower than that. There were times when it went so slowly that you could have walked alongside at a comfortable relaxed pace. Wade figured that we averaged about 15 miles per hour on our 17-hour trip. These days, we were told, that's pretty good time. The situation could get worse, though, as the Russians are proposing to load up the empty grain cars in Churchill with fertilizer for the granaries of Saskatchewan and Manitoba, so there will be heavy freight cars coming and going in both directions.

We slept until about 6:15. Looking at the terrain in the dim morning light we could see that it had changed in a couple of ways: there were no more aspen-like trees, and the land was absolutely flat. The vegetation now took three general forms: moss and low grass, a small leafy deciduous bush about 6 feet tall, and a cedar-like tree about 10 feet tall. If the train had had a second level we could have seen forever. Not much animal life in evidence; so far this morning we have seen only three birds, but no other signs of life. We are told that earlier in the season this place is "all" insects, but they were all gone now. Timing is everything.

A row of tripod-like structures ran parallel to the tracks about 50 feet away. They looked a bit like abandoned teepee frames made of telephone poles. Apparently these once supported telegraph lines that have since been replaced by buried fiberoptic cable put in four years ago. The government awarded a contract to remove the old telegraph lines, but the winning bidder only removed the cable itself, leaving the support tripods.

With a lot of little stops overnight the population had changed, but not increased. We counted 18 passengers in the dining car, eight of whom were workers: four from VIA Rail and four from the freight company. Of the 10 paying passengers, only two were locals. The rest were tourists from other parts of the world. They say that men travel for adventure and women for romance, though I'm not sure that is a sharp distinction as there is a lot of overlap there. Certainly some of my most memorable adventures also involved some romance as well, albeit short-lived. Could be that men and women define romance and adventure differently. The dictionaries on Mars may not read the same as those on Venus.

We went back to our seats and watched the tundra inch by. Our scheduled arrival time had come and gone, and we still had several hours left to go. Everyone had something to read, but I noticed that most had set their books down and just stared out the windows. These unplanned times can produce some of the significant events in our lives. Trying to schedule contemplative moments generally doesn't work. The "aha" experience, the life-changing insight, often occurs when your mind is somewhere (or nowhere) else. For me it was a chance to recalibrate the relative importance of the things I do to occupy my time. I knew that Wade was doing the same thing in his own, even more intensely analytical fashion.

The ride would actually take 19 hours (17 hours of northward motion and a couple of hours going back and forth at Thompson). VIA Canada was sympathetic to the tourists' plight and gave us a free lunch. We had sandwiches as we watched the more or less treeless tundra ooze by. We had expected to see snow, but the land was a kind of gray green, covered with rocks and moss and who knows what else.

It was now after 2 p.m. and our destination was in sight. Happy Birthday to me! September 20 and I turned 62. I quizzed myself on the significance of the anniversary as I stared out the window while the train tiptoed into Churchill. Did I feel old, or at least older? Certainly there was a bit less spring in my step and late-night partying was pretty much out. Other than that, except when I looked at recent photos of myself that provided irrefutable evidence of the ravages of time, I feel pretty much the same as always.

Churchill (named for one of Winston's illustrious ancestors, John Churchill, Duke of Marlborough, a hero of the War of the Spanish Succession) sits on an outcropping of rock, so its citizens don't have to contend with the complications that go along with building on the permafrost that surrounds the town. Complications like heating your house and having it melt into the ground. So Churchill is a real town with paved roads and homes and buildings spread out in all directions. We counted one gas pump, two retail stores, one "sorta" hardware store (Wade couldn't resist—he went in and came out a couple of minutes later to report that something called an analog multimeter [I don't know either] that would cost $6 in Williamsburg was $39 here), and one "sorta" grocery store.

The first European visitor here had been a Danish sea captain who was looking for the elusive Northwest Passage in 1619 and got lost in Hudson Bay (it wasn't called that then). He ran out of provisions near here so he put in for the winter. The crew ate raw meat soaked in vinegar and struggled through a nasty winter that did in 61 out of 64 of them from food poisoning and exposure. The captain and two other sailors survived by eating berries and grass. Restored to health, more or less, they sailed back across the Atlantic in 1620 and were promptly jailed for the crew's death (treacherous times, those). Later he was freed because the Danes needed his seagoing experience. He was getting ready to sail back to "New Denmark" when he died.

We checked our map to locate the Polar Bear B&B that Wade had booked us into. We were told it was a short walk, but I was hesitant. I had heard the stories of polar bears roaming the town, and I wasn't sure I could outrun one of the beasts with or without a suitcase in my hand. Not to worry, I was assured. There was a polar bear patrol that kept them out of town. Those that could not be scared off were tranquilized and put in polar bear jail, which had cells for up to a couple of dozen of them. Well, that made me feel better. Besides, the local boosters went on (why do they never know when to quit?), all of the doors in Churchill were required to be kept unlocked just in case you had to run inside quick to take cover. I was back to being hesitant again.

When I'd moved to bear country in Pennsylvania, I took it upon myself to study up on what to do if I actually stumbled on to one. "Do not try to outrun the bear or climb a tree. They are faster and more agile than you are," all the sources seemed to agree. At that point, the experts diverge. Play dead. Don't play dead. Make a loud noise. Don't be confrontational. No eye contact. Back away. Turn and walk slowly away. Stand still.

I still recall the videos of the supposed expert in Alaska who would camp with the grizzlies and chatter away about the proper way to live among the bears in perfect safety. The cameras were still running as he and his girlfriend got eaten.

Here in Churchill, though, there were people walking around the main drag who seemed unconcerned, so why should I worry? I looked carefully in all directions and headed off behind Wade (who gave no sign that he was the least bit worried about bears) toward our lodgings.

The Polar Bear B&B was not the quaint New England manse one tends to associate with the genre. It was actually a small house that could have been plucked right out of Levittown 50 years ago. A lot of the houses here are prefabs shipped up by rail (we had seen some on a siding). Not sure this was prefab, but it could have been. Our host was a single dad named Donny Gould, with whom Wade had been corresponding for several months. He was a local tugboat captain, ultra-light flying instructor, and general jack-of-all-trades. A restored pick-up truck from the 50s, painted orange and white, was in the driveway, and a handmade observatory hung off the back of the house. We were intrigued to be lodging with Churchill's own Leonardo da Vinci.

Donny had converted one end of the house into three small bedrooms and two baths with showers off a small anteroom. A young German woman said hello as we walked in, but we never saw her again. We had encountered a lot of young women traveling around Canada, many of them working for short periods of time as maids or waitresses to shore up their finances before moving on. We ran into several more in Churchill. There may have been young men doing the same thing, but we didn't encounter them. Perhaps they took outdoor jobs where they were less likely to come into contact with tourists. We didn't know.

Wade took me out for dinner to celebrate my birthday. He and his wife Patty had prepared birthday cards for delivery that night. Our waitress was a charmer from New Zealand who was in Churchill for a few months. The restaurant was a small place, as I guess all of them were. A family with small children carrying balloons walked in. Their son promptly let go of his and it headed up to the highest point in the ceiling, naturally. Another patron and I stacked some tables up and rescued it. Just then the Iowa couple from the train walked in. They had walked around town, seen pretty much what there was to see, and weren't quite sure what to do with themselves next.

As Tanna, the Thompson Tourist Trouble-Shooter (I should get a prize for that string), had told us, we were between seasons—too late for Belugas, too early to see many polar bears. So things were quiet in Churchill, a town of about 1000 souls that would swell to several times that in a few weeks.

The ultimate in land tours around the area are the "tundra buggies," enormous vehicles with huge wheels (and flush toilets) that carried dozens of tourists out across the snow and ice to see the bears. They aren't cheap, each buggy running about $250,000 to buy. The tundra hotels—which looked like a bunch of tundra buggies hooked together but arranged inside with bedrooms, baths, and amenities for $5000 a week—were just being readied to be towed into position.

But, none of them were up and running yet. The man who ran the tundra buggies said if we could get a big enough party together he would crank one up, but that seemed unlikely (interesting guy—wears no socks…I guess to acclimatize himself for Bangkok, Thailand, where he has a house and spends half the year). We had, therefore, arranged to be driven around in a small schoolbus, property of Northstar Tours. Would the folks from Iowa care to join our party? They would.

September 21—Polar Bears

Donny poked his head in about 12:30 a.m. to tell us to come out and see the Northern Lights. I had seen them before and slept through it all, but Wade got up to take a look—his first time, though he had been to some kind of a show in Fairbanks, Alaska. I had assumed that he would have seen plenty of them on his trip to Alaska, but apparently not. So, while I hibernated, he jumped out of bed to take it all in. His report:

"Our host made the announcement with no fan-fare, no big deal for him. Just "the northern lights are out." I got up immediately and saw them at the front door. I moved outside to areas where there was less artificial light and the aurora became brighter. Being new to Churchill, I was imagining a headline like: "conservative republican eaten by polar bear." My plan was that because of the silence, I would at least be able to hear an approaching bear. I finally ended up on the Hudson Bay beach (past the signs warning that it was bear zone and I might get eaten). In the northern sky at about 45 degrees there was a light green band that seemed to flicker and move or wave. It was highest and most definite on my right towards the east. Vertically it took up 25% of the horizon and spanned 120 degrees from right to left. Having been to the northern lights show in Fairbanks, I sorta expected music. In comparison the Fairbanks show was more colorful, but seeing them live and out in the open was far more exhilarating."

The northern lights (aurora borealis) are solar charged particles that collide with the earth's magnetic field. The particles hit the Van Allen belts in the upper atmosphere and "fluoresce" (that means "glow"). Because these belts dip closer to the earth near Churchill, it's a good place to study them; an adjacent military base was originally built for this purpose (actually to study the possibility of using the northern lights as a cold war weapon). Supposedly, the colder the temperature, the more colorful the light show. The unseasonable warmth—around 45 degrees—may explain why the Fairbanks show was more brilliant. Or it may have been digitally enhanced to please the crowd. That's show business.

Wade was still bubbling and filled me in on his nighttime adventure. I, of course, knew nothing about it, and even if I had woken up, I doubt I would have gone tramping around in outer polar bear land at 1 in the morning. Wade had done a quick risk/reward analysis and decided that the light show was worth taking the chance. I would certainly have come to the opposite conclusion.

The "breakfast" part of the Polar Bear Bed and Breakfast consisted of a coupon for the Gypsy Cafe/Bakery, a lively place run by a Portuguese family. It was a pretty simple establishment with a bakery counter down one side where you placed your order and tables everywhere else, but it had a menu that changed every day and the food was pretty good. It was as good as anything we had had lately and, as, a lot of the other places were closed until the next wave of tourists arrived, the Gypsy was where we had all our meals after that.

Rhonda from Northstar Tours picked us up at 9. The Iowa couple, whom we now knew to be Charlie and Dolores Vesely, were already on board. The young German doctor joined us, and off we went with the assurance that we *would* see some polar bears.

Rhonda was what a tour guide should be, handy with answers to the most arcane questions any tourist could dream up, as well as answers to questions about life in these parts that would not occur to anybody from out of town. For example:

- The ground under Churchill was quartzite with silica. Everything looks wet, but Rhonda said the region was actually semi-arid with only about a foot of precipitation per year.

- Most of the rest of the territory is either tundra, taiga (small sticks of trees sticking up), or arboreal forest. Some of the trees have a kind of curious look. They are thin sticks will a ball of green on them, giving them a kind of topiary appearance. That is because the base is protected by snow, but the next section up gets the effect of wind and snow and is "snow blasted clean" The remainder is shaped by wind alone.

- We saw a couple of polar bears. She said they were a mother and a son. The mother kept her distance because the son was about 3 years old and ready to be kicked out to fend for himself. The bears don't like wind apparently, and don't eat until they get on the ice, so they don't hunt much on land. I wanted some pictures of myself with bears in the background to send to the local paper, but Rhonda wouldn't let us get close enough for a good shot (Rhonda has dealt with camera-happy tourists before, obviously). They're not as far away as you think they are, she said, and they are very fast. So we used a zoom on the bears, and I had to settle for a posed shot in front of some polar bear statues back in town. The local paper back home was satisfied and ran it.

- About 300 bears and 3000 Belugas pass through Churchill each year. We had come believing time was running out and that we had best see the bears now before they were all gone. Well, if they are an endangered species word hasn't reached Churchill yet. The general health of the bears has been improving, as has their fecundity; the birth rate has improved from one every three years to up to three. Same for the Belugas—there are now so many that they have nearly fished the bay clean.

- The town took over an old military building to store its garbage. They used to incinerate, but the device was too small and did a poor job. What didn't burn attracted bears, so now they put their trash in the building and lock it up behind reinforced steel. What happens when it is full—who knows?

- We passed a long low ruined building. It had been an above-ground tunnel through which rockets were transported from the assembly building to the launch site. The rockets had been used to study the Van Allen belts. Some jerk had torn the building apart for the plywood and left the insulation blowing in the wind.

- A local guy named George had smoked cigars for most of his 90 years. When the province passed no-smoking rules that applied to the Canadian Legion hall where George spent most of his time smoking and playing slot machines, they made a special exception in his case. When he died, they cremated him and buried his ashes in a money bag.

- The ubiquitous piles of stones dotting the landscape that vaguely resemble a human figure are called inukshuks and were used for guideposts and message posts by the Indians. A local citizen decided that arrangements of large stones, including inukshuks, would dress up the town, which cannot support gardens, fountains, and the like, so he built a bunch of these things. He also arranged boulders at various places, partly for show and partly to discourage ATVs from running in between the buildings and tearing up the place.

- The polar bears that cannot be chased away with noise and firecrackers are shot with dart guns and airlifted by helicopter to the polar bear jail. There were eight bears in the lock-up when we drove past. They sit there with no food for a couple of months and are then released. They get no food and are kept in isolation in cinder block cells because their jailers don't want them to get comfortable and come back. Isolation means no visitors, including camera-toting tourists. We saw signs all around town that identified bear no-go zones, similar to the ones Wade had ignored in his quest to get a better view of the aurora.

- Rhonda took us down to the port. There were several barges being loaded there. A number of towns along the coast get their supplies by barge from Churchill. Each town has its own barge, and it gets filled up and shipped out once a month. The port and the hospital are the town's largest employers, at least during the off season. When the tourists come to town from October to December the population swells from 1,100 to over 3000. (When the military base and research facility were running, the town may have had as many as 5000 people.)

- The grain elevator, by far the largest structure in town, was built in pieces. Nearby there are a number of shacks called Jocktown. The workers didn't want to have deductions from their wages for lodging so they built the shacks, some of which are still in use.

- From the hill near Jocktown you can look out over the river across to the fort built by the Hudson Bay Company in the 1600s at the mouth of the Churchill River. The fort fed a community of Indians, but it was attacked by the French who drove the English out. The French did not care for the Indians, so many died.

- The water in town is heated—the trees that grow above the pipeline are among the youngest but also the biggest in the area as a result. Electricity is included in the rent—most houses are rented from Manitoba Power—because if one froze, the water for heating would get cut off to the others in the group and they would freeze too.

- A surprising feature is a 26,000-foot runway. It had been 32,000 feet but 6000 feet caved in. The remaining runway is long enough to land pretty much anything, including the space shuttle, so a lot of over-the-pole flights are routed over Churchill, just in case. Some of the old military base has been taken over by something called the Northern Studies Institute, but most of the base along with a lot of old equipment sits idle.

- One of the things about the tundra is that it can't hide much. Clear air and the lack of trees exposes things that didn't go right. Like "Miss Piggy," the plane wreck that sits out by the airport, and the ship that was supposedly scuttled by Onassis on its last run and that lies beached just outside town.

Rhonda drove us past her house for a look at her husband's Silverado. He was so protective of it that he seldom drove it, lest it get dirty or dinged. We swung around the town center – a long building that contains a hospital, library, athletic facilities including a swimming pool, meeting rooms—all connected so one never had to brave the elements to get from one to another.

We coasted into the parking lot at Northstar Tours just as the bus ran out of gas—the second time for me in a week. The second time for me in 40 years. The town is small enough, however, that you can easily hoof it from one end to the other—carefully avoiding the polar bear no-go areas, of course.

Time for a drink. At the Canadian Legion we met up again with Charlie and Dolores Vesely. Dolores and I played slots while Charlie and Wade chatted over drinks. The place was packed and full of very friendly folks. I was beginning to think I could live in this place. Some of the friendly folks were taken with my $8 day-glo orange parka and just had to come over and check it out. I wasn't sure if they really admired it or not. Then Wade started to laugh and they laughed, too…and then I was sure. It wasn't admiration.

Back to the Gypsy for dinner and a chat with the owner's young nephew, who was in from Portugal for a few months to work on his English and his restauranting skills before going back home to make a formal study of the food business at a culinary school.

September 22—Last Day in Churchill

We were back at the Gypsy for breakfast. Not too busy, so Mrs. De Silva had time to talk about her childhood in Portugal. Her family had moved from Lisbon to Montreal and then on to Churchill. Her nephew from Portugal, whom we had chatted with before, had planned to go back home at the end of the summer, but was enjoying himself and extended his stay until the end of bear season in the middle of November. For such a small town, Churchill attracted a lot of young people from all over. They seemed to have no trouble finding short-term jobs as waiters and waitresses or in cleaning guest rooms. One of the European girls on our train took a cleaning job for a day to augment her travel money. Our B&B was being cleaned by a young woman I took to be Japanese.

I popped into the Eskimo Museum which, though small, had enough to hold my interest for over an hour. Lots of carvings representing Indian legends, tools, stuffed animals, and exhibits on the history of the area. There were artifacts from Inuit, Cree, and Dene, the most interesting of which to me were the ivory carvings that illustrated folk tales and myths. The whole story could be held in the palm of your hand.

Outside, I bumped into Father Albert, the Roman Catholic priest. I had heard from a number of people what a wonderful man he was. No question he was friendly. I learned that he had a twin sister, as I have, that he was from Alberta, and that he had a fascination with reading and words—as I have. I suspect that living in a small place that gets smaller in the winter, and darker and colder at the same time, reading can be pretty important.

I mused some more about what it would be like to live in this place. Maybe I could do it—I thought about opening a soup and sandwich place. Pure fantasy, of course, but who knows.

I said goodbye to Father Albert and moseyed over to the Anglican Church, also presided over by a popular priest, Father Charles. Because finding building materials in Churchill was as much a problem in the 1890s as today, many of them were shipped in then as now. The church was sort of a kit, with the iron frame of the building prefabbed in England and sent over. I recall Rhonda telling us that it had originally been on the other side of the river and was then moved.

I checked out the Churchill Public Library one last time. Wade and I used it every day to catch up on the news and word from back home. We have not watched TV and there is no cell phone service here, but the Internet access via fiberoptic cable is good. Lots of kids from the school next door come in and out—this is the school library, too. Makes a lot of sense, particularly in such a small community. The librarian, a charming woman with what I took to be a German accent (like I would know), had moved up to Churchill with her husband years ago to stay for 2 months, then 3 more, then... they raised their kids here, who are now in Winnipeg and Phoenix and don't visit much. I sensed that her work in an area that attracted so many children filled a hole for her.

I caught up with Wade outside—we spent some portion of our extravehicular time in solitary exploration—and he had a new discovery to show me. Just east of the community center, and past another "bear zone" warning sign, was the beginnings of a structure known locally as the "Rock Hotel." Started in 2002, 70% of the foundation of the building is done, but that's it. It reminded me of Machu Pichu in Peru, where the carefully fitted stone foundations and walls were all that remained of the Inca village. This could have been a small village; it was big enough. The place is being constructed in fits and starts with government grant money. Needless to say, that in and of itself is the source of some controversy.

We took one more walk around town, then headed off for dinner at the Gypsy again. We chatted with some guys from Manitoba Telecom we had met earlier—there was a big group of them in town working on the phone lines. Important up here—a place with no cell phone service relies pretty heavily on its land lines.

The train to Thompson left at 8:30 p.m.. We ate the last of the cookies Patty Swink had sent along with us, a custom with Wade and Patty that I enjoyed being part of this trip. It reminded Wade once again of his trip to Alaska. He had eaten the last of her chocolate chip cookies in Fairbanks.

Wade was finishing up the C.S. Lewis book and was feeling philosophical. "...the things I assert most vigorously are the things I resisted long and accepted late" Lewis says on page 213. While Wade got into this book at the recommendation of male friends of his as way of showing him someone who had found religion late in life, it also showed him someone who came to a point where he made a major change in direction. "...it is one thing to see the land from a wooded ridge and another to trek the road that leads to it" (page 230).

"Whether sitting on the Yukon River at Dawson City a few years back or riding this train, being physically removed from taxes, maintenance, and day-to-day responsibilities lets me see things better and feel differently. I have a new understanding that the simple life makes me a better person" (Wade Swink, VIA Rail dining car).

Maybe it was just as well there was no cell phone service in Churchill. Just think of what we might have come up with if there had been no Internet either.

September 23—Back in Thompson

The train seemed to be moving faster this time, but it was mostly illusory as our time back to Thompson was no better than it had been coming. We may have spent less time going back and forth in the train yard, so perhaps the speed on the tracks was not my imagination after all.

We had breakfast with Charlie and Dolores Vesely. I had pancakes with piles of blueberries on them. Obviously breakfast was the chef's (a woman this time) best thing. We teased the Veselys about our plan to descend on them on the way back. To our surprise, they didn't laugh it off and seemed to like the idea. Allrighty then, it's a date.

A young man at the next table was a teacher in Churchill (185 students from 1st to 11th grade)—a position heavily subsidized with housing allowance and other perks ($5200 for housing and a $3000 northern allowance). He taught physical education and tourism, of all things, and had just come back from a tourism seminar. Probably the counterpart of shop class in a factory town.

As the train neared civilization, my cell phone came to life again and I was able to catch up on things back home. Charles' (my partner) medical tests had come back favorably—the triglyceride medicine appeared to be working. My cousin from Colorado, however, had advanced from prostate cancer to bladder problems and the first signs of renal failure, so it didn't look good. His daughter had been given a more positive prognosis, so she had gone ahead with a trip to Europe. Her dad would die while she was away. Things took the course of so many of my hospitalized friends who had been prepared for the best and had suffered the worst. I wondered if the doctors practiced positive spins as a psychological tool, or if they were dealing with events they really didn't understand. Recent experience confirmed the opinion I had formed during my days as an orderly when I was in college—stay away from hospitals as much as possible.

Colleen and her grandson from McCreedy Park picked us up from the Thompson station. Back at the camper I decided my hair was getting a bit shaggy so I pulled out the clippers I had brought along and did some pruning. I guess I missed a pretty big spot because Wade felt it was worth razzing me about.

We headed off to Wal-Mart to download our pictures on a disk to free up space for more pictures. Not that we were taking all that many. I tend to get absorbed by my surroundings and only later think "that would have made a great picture." I vow to be more disciplined in the future, a promise that rolls easily off the tongue and one I have made so many times before.

September 24—On to Saskatchewan

Next morning we made another stop at Wal-Mart, this time to pick up something to keep me warm at night. While I have tended not to feel the cold during the day, at some point during the night (when temperatures got down in the 20s) the thin comforter and sheet on me left me feeling exposed and shivering. Wade seems to be able to get by with a sheet and a blanket and not much else. So, I picked up a comforter and another pillow. From now on all would be warm and snuggly.

Heading south we made a breakfast stop at Wabowden in a new log building that was built, as was all the furniture inside, by the owner's brother. I had Ma's secret recipe pancakes, which were excellent, and reviewed the family pictures on the walls.

We turned off Route 6 at Ponton and headed for Saskatchewan under dark skies. Gassed up at Bearberry Portage. The sign said "no more than 4 customers in store at any one time." We goofed with a very nice Jamaican woman in the store by peeking our heads in and counting the number of customers—there weren't any. I guess we weren't the first; she laughed and waved us in. She said the owner had put up the sign—she had no idea why.

The country turned hilly and we entered a rocky area (something called greenstone) that looked like the badlands. We were in Flin Flon, a huge (and I mean huge) mining complex with enormous mining and processing installations that handled gold, copper, and nickel. Flin Flon was one of those places where the name so intrigued us that a stop was imperative.

For lunch we chose Mugsy's, no longer run by Mugsy but by a woman named Linda who was greeter, waitress, cook, dishwasher and cashier. And, if the place is not too busy, she appears to do all of them well (sometimes her mother helps). We struck up a conversation with a couple at another table who told us that the town was named for a fictional character—Josiah Flintabbatey Flonatin, Flin Flon for short—who traveled around in an underground submarine and surfaced in strange places. One such place was described in *The Sunless City*...a land of gold dust. Prospectors who found gold in 1914 had apparently read the book and named their claim, and subsequently the town, for its hero. Al Capp, of L'il Abner fame, was fascinated by this and created a drawing of Mr. Flin Flon, which was turned into a 24-foot statue. (This was the second town we had been in that had memorialized Mr. Capp in one way or another. In his day he had been the hottest cartoonist/satirist/lecturer/radio personality around and was always one of my favorites. Now he is barely remembered, at least in most of the United States. Don't know if it was changing times or political correctness—remember he made advances to a young woman while touring college campuses—that did him in.)

We pulled into the local co-op in Flin Flon for some groceries and then got gas and info a short hop away at Creighton, Saskatchewan. There was an old Pontiac Phoenix sitting outside the chamber information office. It was one of the General Motors X cars built in the early '80s that was supposed to roll back the Japanese auto invasion. X cars were so poorly made (and ugly) that they had the opposite effect and are real rarities—you never see one at an antique car show. I had to take a picture of it, which may have unsettled its owner —a young man using one of the computers inside. I felt bad but didn't know how to apologize without explaining what my fascination with the clunker was.

Our next gas stop was a hundred something miles down the road at a service area that was full of people eating lunch on vouchers—some kind of local welfare.

Camp for the night was at Narrow Hills, about 70–80 kilometers from Prince Albert. It was 28 degrees, our coldest night yet, but with my new comforter (plus the old one, Wade reminds me), I was quite warm.

Wade and I talked about a deceased friend of his who might still be around if a cooler head had been calling the shots while he was in the hospital. Not the first time I have heard someone emphasize the importance of having a medical advocate. He borrowed my cell phone and called Patty, who was heading down to the Outer Banks of North Carolina for a Bible retreat. I may have mentioned that her adoption of the local megachurch was one of Wade's motivations for his religious introspective.

CANADA
ÉTATS-UNIS
ALASKA (E.U.)
GROENLAND (Danemark)
ISLANDE
REYKJAVIK
MER DE BEAUFORT
BAIE DE BAFFIN
BAIE D'HUDSON
BASSIN FOXE
OCÉAN PACIFIQUE
OCÉAN ATLANTIQUE
TERRE-NEUVE
Détroit de Davis
Détroit d'Hudson
Cercle polaire arctique
TERRITOIRES DU NORD OUEST
DISTRICT DE MACKENZIE
DISTRICT DE KEEWATIN
DISTRICT DE FRANKLIN
YUKON
COLOMBIE BRITANNIQUE
ALBERTA
SASKATCHEWAN
MANITOBA
ONTARIO
QUÉBEC
NOUVEAU BRUNSWICK
N.lle ÉCOSSE
CÔTE DU LABRADOR
ILE DE BANKS
ILE VICTORIA
ILE DEVON
I. Stefansson
I. Disko
Ile Southampton
I. Coats
I. Mansel
Iles Belcher
I. Résolution
I. Akpatok
I. Anticosti
Iles de la Reine Charlotte
Ile Vancouver
Péninsule d'Ungava
Baie d'Ungava
Baie de James
G. de Boothia
Golfe d'Amundsen
D.t de Lancaster
D.t de Belle Isle
G. du St Laurent
C. Farewell
C. Chidley
C. Dorset
C. Sable
C. Cod
Monts Mackenzie
Monts Selwyn
Monts Ogilvie
Mts Cassiar
Mt St Elie
Plateau du Yukon
Cascades
Lac Supérieur
Lac Michigan
Lac Huron
L. Ontario
L. Winnipeg
L. Athabasca
L. Nueltin
L. Dubawnt
Whitehorse
Dawson
Forty Mile
Aklavik
Port Brabant (Tuktoyaktuk)
Coppermine
Port Radium
Yellowknife
Ft Simpson
Ft Nelson
Prince Rupert
Kitimat
Kemano
Port Alice
Port Alberni
VICTORIA
VANCOUVER
Kamloops
Vernon
Kelowna
Penticton
Nelson
Trail
Jasper
EDMONTON
CALGARY
Red Deer
Lethbridge
Medicine Hat
SASKATOON
REGINA
Moose Jaw
Swift Current
Weyburn
Estevan
Prince Albert
North Battleford
Yorkton
Brandon
WINNIPEG
St Boniface
Churchill
York Factory
Eskimo Point
Kenora
Port Arthur
Ft William
Sault Ste Marie
Sudbury
North Bay
Timmins
Kapuskasing
Cochrane
Moosonee
OTTAWA
Kingston
Brockville
TORONTO
Hamilton
London
Windsor
DETROIT
Niagara Falls
St Catharines
MONTRÉAL
QUÉBEC
Trois Rivières
Sherbrooke
Chicoutimi
Sept-Iles
Schefferville
Goose Bay
Nain
Hopedale
Frobisher Bay
Pangnirtung
Pond Inlet
Clyde
Thulé
Craig Harbour
Edmundston
St JEAN
HALIFAX
Sydney
Corner Brook
St JEAN
Miquelon
St Pierre (Fr.)
PORTLAND
BOSTON
NEW YORK
Long Island
Mississippi
Columbia
Yellowstone
Yukon

September 25—Green Peas Don't Make Good Soup

From Narrow Hills we took the road to Prince Albert, passing a lake with thousands of snow geese so we stopped for pictures. Several other cars followed us off the highway, blocking the road for some large trucks with much annoyed looking drivers.

The land had changed from hilly conifer forests to open fields and farms. We saw signs to Batoche, site of the battle with the Metis. We had heard of neither, so naturally we turned off onto a badly chewed up road—in some places the pavement was barely discernible—to take a look.

Some miles down the messy road we passed a restaurant in a tiny hamlet called Ile De Bellevue. Outside there was a little model village and a statue that looked a bit like a tree. We backtracked and went into the Cultural Center. The statue was of a pea plant, green pods and all—of course we took a picture of it. I asked if they had pea soup for lunch. "Of course" the charming little lady said. Turns out we were in the pea capital of Saskatchewan. She brought us bowls of hot brown soup—looked a bit like lentil. "I thought pea soup was green," I said innocently. Without missing a beat she looked over her shoulder and retorted "Green peas don't make good soup!"

Well, the soup was good, all right, as were the pork chops and potatoes that came with it. Wade rated it 1 of 5 top meals of the trip, my first awareness of how serious he was about ranking things.

Down the road in Batoche we came to the Batoche Visitors Center, a very imposing place with a museum, multimedia show, and an impressively sized staff. We were told to hurry and catch up with the tour group, so we hotfooted it several hundred yards down the hill to a church where a docent was feeding history to a group of restless teenagers. We went next door to a restored parsonage and school where another tour leader picked up the story.

We let the kids go on and hung around to talk to one of the guides who told us the story of the Metis, of whom he was one. The Metis were mixed bloods, part Indian, part European (French trappers) who had a pretty prosperous settlement going. A dispute arose over land, involving the Meti system of assigning river lots, versus a square township system used by much of the rest of the country (presumably an Anglo system). In any case, title to the land became problematic and the Metis felt their interests were not being represented in Ottawa, so they invited a man who had spearheaded a rights movement in Manitoba to come in and lead them. The dispute turned into an armed struggle in 1885, culminating in a couple of battles with first the Mounties at Duck Lake (the Metis won) and a month later with the Canadian Army (the Metis lost). Twenty-five people died, the ringleader was hanged, and Batoche almost disappeared into obscurity. Now, however, the place is being restored as a National Historic Site and there is this big fancy Visitors Center (due to be remodeled yet) staffed by personable sorts who are eager to talk to visitors who are genuinely interested in the history of the place (that would be us) rather than horsing around with nubile teens of opposite sexes on a school field trip who have other things on their minds. So, we were treated to private tours and lectures from Ron, Linda, Rachelle, and Lee, who left us with the impression that there were still Metis around and they hadn't forgotten.

Wade was intrigued by the encounter and wondered what the United States would look like if there had been a greater French influence. Coming from just up the road from Yorktown, he was mindful of the French role in the American Revolution. "Comparing the British and French colonies in 1700 vs. now, the French colonies are not as successful. The difference may be that the French, like the Metis, resisted change and were determined to maintain their lifestyles and traditions no matter what, even if it meant fighting a continuous string of losing battles."

We had dinner at the Mandarin Restaurant in Saskatoon, where we were given far more to eat than we could handle, then headed south in search of a campground with a hot shower. We failed to find one and ended up beside a lake at the Blackstrap Camp in Dundurn.

September 26—Moose Jaw

Up at dawn to watch white and black ducks and a lone otter meander around the lake. Wade and I talked about Islam and my sister the Muslim. Although I grew up in Muslim countries, and can certainly understand the pull of tradition, I had a harder time understanding the allure of Islam for converts who grew up in the West. There is something to be said, I suppose, for the relative security of a faith that hasn't changed much over the centuries, as opposed to mainstream Christian religions that embrace theological change more readily and enthusiastically. Logically, if one chooses a religion because its teachings most closely reflects the will of God, what does it say when those teachings change. Did God change his mind? Did our earlier principles not accurately represent what he wanted of us? Are we just guessing (or worse, making it up)? Are we better guessers now, or were we better guessers then? Or, do we simply have no idea? The beauty of an unchanging fundamentalism is that it does not trouble itself with these uncertainties. That avoids a lot of confusion on the part of its adherents, but you have to adhere first. That's where I always had my difficulties, and that also seemed to be where Wade was getting stuck.

We drove to Moose Jaw and consulted with the Canadian Automobile Association about our route. Then off to the Polar Bear Confectionary and Laundromat to slim down the growing pile of dirty clothes in the camper closet. The combination of washing machines and ice cream freezers was not as curious as you might think. I took charge of the laundry and then went outside and savored a strawberry ice cream cone while Wade sat in the sun in a tee shirt wiggling his bare feet reading three current newspapers. "Is this not great!!" he shouted to the world, though he was looking at me. Must have been—he left his papers and diary behind, and we had to turn around and visit the place again to retrieve them.

The name of the place, the Polar Bear, prompted a discussion with the young proprietors. Once again we encountered people who were surprised that we had been to Churchill. Those who actually knew where it was echoed the sentiments we had heard so many times before—they really had always wanted to make the trip.

The afternoon was spent lolling in the mineral spa at Temple Gardens —named for Mr. and Mrs. Temple's dance hall of some generations earlier. A different time…Mrs. Temple used to patrol the dance floor to separate couples she thought were dancing too close. We lunched at Harwood's Restaurant in the spa.

We rented a campsite south of town at a place called River Park, which like the others we had visited was also just about to close for the season. Then back up to the north of town to a Visitors Center that had an enormous statue of a moose outside. Mac the Moose was coming apart and was partly fenced off. We donated to a collection to restore him—he had already had surgery on his jaw, but more needed to be done. We also bought some touristy T-shirts for the cause.

At around 4 p.m. we were heading back east toward the campground when a man in a pick-up truck on our right turned to his left in front of us and signaled for us to stop. He rolled his window down and said that he had been behind us for several blocks and noticed that our left rear duals were wobbling. We had driven over 4000 miles like this without noticing anything, but he was insistent. We said thanks and pulled over to check. Sure enough, I drove slowly and Wade saw the wobble. We went to the local Toyota dealer and made an appointment for the next morning.

Dinner was a disappointing—and cold—moussaka at the Mad Greek. Once again my instincts had failed me, and I had picked a loser. I actually had to send my dinner back because it was too cold to eat.

We went back to River Park, where Wade spent a restless night going over various scenarios on the camper: broken axle, bad wheel bearings, and worse...we fly home and he comes back later to pick it up.

September 27—Back to the States

Next morning we spoke to Bill Shiers, who with his wife owned the River Park Camp, which he called the oldest continuously operating camp in North America. It has been in operation since 1927—but only had some tents and a kitchen during the Depression. Bill came out from Nova Scotia as a cowboy. Since then he and his wife had six kids, including two sets of twins.

Bill said no on the Toyota dealer and said we should take the camper to his mechanic, Constables on Manitoba Street. Good recommendation. Dale and his son Scott quickly found and fixed the problem. A portion of the valve stem extension was wedged between the duals' mating flanges. Solution: remove it and the wheels lined up smartly. The bill for having the wheels repaired and oil changed would come to $73.

While Wade waited around the garage, I took a walking tour of the town. Nice place, obviously very into downtown restoration, with a restored theater and a number of restaurants, but no fast food. The Centennial Park across from the Temple Gardens spa had a bunch of swans and warning signs to keep your distance—apparently they can have ugly tempers.

Ask where the name Moose Jaw comes from and you can count on a different answer from everybody you talk to. They will generally agree that it stems from an Indian word, they just can't agree on which one: the word that means the river that runs through town is shaped like a Moose Jaw; the word that describes an event involving an actual Moose Jaw; the word that means "warm breezes".... Everyone had a favorite version.

I arrived back at Constables as they were finishing up work on the camper. A woman had brought in her '73 Oldsmobile hardtop convertible for servicing. One of the brothers, who is of an age with me, came out, and we reminisced about the old days of cruising along in one of these things. A young mechanic came out to listen and was surprised when we told him that the gas mileage in those days wasn't a whole lot worse than what most cars get these days. My '64 Chevy used to get in the low 20s.

Wade and I walked a block or two away to the National Cafe where a full breakfast was only $2.99. We had driven by here the night before but it had offered a Chinese buffet, and we were not ready for more Chinese so we had regrettably gone Greek. We talked to the owner who said it had been a Chinese restaurant until a couple of years ago when he retired from the insurance business and went into the restaurant business, partly so his daughter would have something to do. Chinese is popular here, and the old cook had stayed on to do dinners. The place was full of pictures, mostly of the states and many of Colonial Williamsburg, so Wade felt right at home. A movie company had done a film there, substituting Moose Jaw for New Jersey. They had used his restaurant as a diner set and paid him $20,000 and repainted the place.

Wade, relieved that the mechanical problem this morning had been resolved so painlessly, reflected on his good fortune. "This was as simple a problem as it could have possibly been," he said. "A number of events came together to produce this great outcome. First we were stopped by a total stranger and told about the wobble. There was no sign from the inside of this problem such as vibration. Second, the campground's owner intercepted us before we took off for the Toyota dealer and sent us to Constables instead. Third, although the folks at Constables had no direct experience with Class C RVs, they were experienced problem solvers and knew just how to approach it. Do I deserve to be so lucky? Why do some people have most of the accidents and all of the bad luck?"

Implicit in this monologue was the suggestion that he *did* deserve to be lucky and that the others who had most of the accidents did not.

Still, he maintained that we had met four kind people for every "sour" person we had encountered on our trip. I would have placed the ratio higher than that. Sour was harsh judgment in Wade's book. "There are no EVIL people" he insists, a position I took issue with several times, having known a few evil people in my time and read about lots more. One of the good things about our relationship is that we are comfortable, usually, with differences of opinion. I cannot say that about all of my acquaintances, some of whom regard it as a personal affront when one does not embrace their point of view. Religion and politics mostly, of course, but I have been given the silent treatment over movies and restaurants, too. Life's too short.

After breakfast we drove south toward the U.S. border. There were vast stretches of farmland and every so often a complex of farm buildings surrounded by trees. Some had rows of old wooden buildings that I thought might have been for migrant workers.

There was no line at the U.S. border. On the Canadian side there was just a sign that said "proceed to U.S." On the U.S. side there were two very pleasant border patrolmen, one a just-retired sergeant major with 23 years in the Army. They were much more welcoming toward two old Army vets than their Canadian counterparts had been when we crossed the border going north 15 days earlier.

We crossed over and drove to Plentywood, Montana. Once again a fascinating name caused us to stop. Whence the name? The story goes that a bunch of cowboys and a cook were attempting to build a fire out of buffalo chips. Old Dutch Henry came along and told them

"If you'll go a couple of miles up this creek, you'll find plenty wood." Believe it or not.

We had lunch at Cousins, which was pretty much full the whole time we were there. I ordered a "medium burger," which stopped the waitress in her tracks. "A hamburger cooked medium" I translated. That cleared things up. I was relieved to find that we were back in the land of cheap gas, inasmuch as I was buying the stuff.

The area was undergoing something of an oil boom, and we were to pass lots of oil wells in Montana. We also noticed a lot of people with really big guts, something we had not seen the whole time we were in Canada. Anybody who believes the obesity thing is not cultural should crisscross the border and see how much difference a few miles make.

We stopped in Williston, North Dakota, to check out tourist information and look for a place to camp. We passed several multiplex cinemas right in town—unusual—before we finally found the town hall where we got some local brochures. We decided to press on to Watford City, some 40 miles south. On the way we passed the confluence of the Missouri and Yellowstone Rivers. Wade had devoured the accounts of the Lewis and Clark expeditions and was pretty excited to come across some of the geography that featured in their annals—this alone made the trip worth it, he said.

Camp for the night was in the Watford City Park, where we got water, power, and showers for $10 a night. We stocked up on groceries at the local market and settled in, or tried to. The site was a bit noisy with an airport and fairgrounds just south of us. I called home and found that Charles had backed his car into a tree.

September 28—The Center of the Continent

We gassed up again in Watford City, then again in Bowman, crossing the Little Missouri as we went. The only place to eat in town was a place called the #3, which was being remodeled. Actually there weren't that many places in town to do anything, it being a rather small community. And there was lots of open space from one small community to the next. Sort of reminded me of somebody's description of...Kansas, I think: "miles and miles of miles and miles." I was to think of this again when we drove across western Nebraska.

Our tour took us through what purported to be the geographic center of the continent, which includes Canada and Alaska, near Belle Fourche, French for "beautiful fork," a description of the joining of two rivers. How do they know this is the geographic center of North America? We did some checking and found that a town called Rugby, North Dakota, also makes this claim and that we were about 20 miles away from the so-called "center of the geographic land mass of the United States (including Alaska)." Again, how do they know? The state of North Dakota says:

> The U.S. Geological Survey does not recognize the geographic center of North America (or that of the 50 States or the

conterminous United States) as exact locations. The reason for this is that there is no generally accepted definition of a geographic center and no reliable way of determining it. Consequently there are probably as many geographic centers of a given area as there are definitions.

A little farther south we landed in Spearfish, South Dakota. With some effort, we were able to find the local AAA office, which was carefully hidden on a side road next to a carwash. Despite their best efforts, however, we could not find a place for me to get an ice cream cone (I get cravings).

So we pressed on into the Badlands and then the Black Hills, which were more beautiful than I remembered despite the fact that the area was experiencing a very obvious drought. The land was quite dry, the bodies of water we passed were quite low, and the hills around Deadwood were charred from a major forest fire. Things were jumping in the towns, though, which were full of new casinos. Seemed like every motel had its own.

We passed Lead, home of Homestake Mine. Most of the campsites and visitors centers had closed for the season. We found one part of the Pactola National Park campsite open and stopped there for the night. We had the place entirely to ourselves.

September 29—The Black Hills

I suppose it was inevitable that at some point the relative amicability and sunniness of the journey might run into at least one brief rain cloud. From my perspective (you can ask Wade for his) there was only one. On the whole, we are long-time friends who can talk candidly about anything, and I mean anything. We had discussed politics and religion, of course; that was to be expected. But the discussions covered a wider swath and got into remarkable detail. Old cars, global warming, children, sea levels past and present, ancient civilizations, personal relationships, and "what are you doing with the rest of your life."

It was the last of these that caused the brief and happily short-lived flare up. I had finished outlining my plans for the future, which included possibly volunteering to work on a political campaign of someone I thought worth working for (again after many years, my last active involvement having been the John Anderson campaign of 1980), having some of my songs recorded, finishing some books I had been working on for quite a while, and continuing my volunteer work at a lower level than in the preceding decade. In conversations that began the night before and continued into this morning, Wade proposed that he regarded these pursuits to be a waste of time and that "all of my successful friends have drive, and you don't."

I was not sure if I had said something earlier that had upset him, or if he was out of sorts, or if his opinion of me was somewhat lower than I had been led to suspect. Whatever the case, his remarks killed the conversation for the better part of the day, while I brooded and mulled things over.

By day's end, I had decided to let him know I was a little pissed (which he knew already) then move on. I concluded that, first of all, while there are many definitions of success and I do not regard myself in any way as a failure, he was probably talking about financial success, and it was certainly true that this had never been much of a motivator for me. I had always lived well and had enough resources to do pretty much whatever I wanted, and I was reasonably confident that my life would continue that way at least for the next decade or so. I also realized that I was in many ways the antithesis of the classic "driven man." So many of the people I know, and probably most of the ones Wade knows, come closer to this model, so his observation about drive was probably not far off. Finally, I decided that a friend of 40 years who had a reputation for bluntness—a quality I had always found refreshing in the past—was entitled to the benefit of the doubt.

So, after thinking about it for a day during which we took separate personal tours of Mt. Rushmore (which both of us had been to before), I chose to brighten up and forget the whole thing. Wade said later that he thought Teddy Roosevelt was out of place with the other "great" presidents. Supposedly, the sculptor admired him for seeing the Panama Canal through.

We had lunch in a very touristy Keystone at a place called the Buffalo Bar. Wade had buffalo chili that he thought was pretty good. I had some kind of grilled sandwich the components of which I don't remember. We drove into Nebraska and across some of the most unremarkable landscape—save for its vast emptiness—that I have seen since North Africa. Wade said it was the first time he had been bored on the whole trip. As we came into the eastern end of the state we also came back into contact with trees and greenery.

We were impressed with the omnipresence of huge grain silos. There had been grain silos in Canada, too, but there they were mostly concrete, like windowless skyscrapers on the horizon every ten miles apart. The ones we encountered in Nebraska and Iowa were more metallic and newer looking. Obviously the price of corn and soy was going up, powered at least in part by the ethanol boom. Lots of new ethanol plants, too (doubt if there are a lot of old ones around, but I could be wrong). All in all, this part of the country looked pretty prosperous, but it also looked like there had been more people living here at one time than there were now.

We passed through several towns that had the word "sand" in their names or in the names of the bar in the center of town. These towns were less prosperous looking, and we noticed that the soil around them was indeed sandy.

In Valentine we found a campsite behind a motel at the far end of town (site #33, $23). The place was run by a woman from Estonia and her American husband. At first, he seemed pretty chilly, but when I saw him later with his grandchildren he couldn't have been more pleasant. There didn't seem to be a lot of business in the motel part, but the camp part was pretty full. Most of the sites seemed to be taken up with permanent residents. They had lawn furniture and large propane gas tanks outside.

There were a couple of large restaurants in town. The Peppercorn came highly recommended, so we decided to give it a try. We parked across the street as a storm was slowly pushing into town. A middle-aged man came up to us and engaged Wade in conversation. Wade is pretty open with everyone. Then the man asked him for money. Without missing a beat, Wade said he would see him on the way out, by which time he was gone – perhaps discouraged by the storm.

It was good to see how many young people were at the restaurant when we walked in. The steakhouse in the center of town was big and packed. And I would say half the people there were under 30, maybe younger than that. Always good to see young people out having a good time, especially so in an area that I had believed was losing its young to the bright lights of the city and aging fast.

Well, almost always. We had seen a lot of finger flipping, high beaming, and swearing by young men (and some young women) as they drove around and were in some perceived way inconvenienced by other drivers or pedestrians. Impatient and angry, and maybe a bit tipsy as well (it was a weekend, after all), carfuls of loud, menacing youngsters can make one watchful and a bit nervous. One older woman in a car by herself had looked a bit shaken when she was harassed for pulling away from a light too slowly.

Wade and I went back to the camper and both watched a major thunderstorm pass over. Lots of lightning and dark clouds, but not all that much rain. We had our first shower since Moose Jaw and called it a day.

September 30—Iowa

We had breakfast at the Buckhorn restaurant in town and swapped pleasantries with a very cheerful octogenarian at the cash register. A model for us all, she was coming close to the end of her life and couldn't have been happier. My guess is that even though she was working on Sunday morning, there was a strong underpinning of faith and family shoring her up.

The landscape changed as we drove further into eastern Nebraska— less sand, more trees and terracing. We had not seen terracing anywhere else in this country before and did not know that the practice, so common in other parts of the world, was in use here in the States.

We crossed the Missouri into Iowa and followed the signs for the visitors center in Sioux City. The signs that had been so prominent on the highway disappeared pretty quickly, and we never did find the place. We gave up and headed back to the main road.

A while further we stopped for gas and lunch in Moville, asking some local folks if they could recommend a good place to eat. They couldn't, because all the restaurants closed at 1 p.m. on Sundays—for miles around. So we ate in the A&W and headed on to Fort Dodge, passing through Correctionville on the way. Always fascinated with names, I checked later to find out that Correctionville (the longest single city name in Iowa—how's that for a distinction), was not named for a prison, as I had guessed, but for a surveying correction line that runs east to west through the center of town. It corrects for the roundness of the earth to make land parcels the same size. Practically, the correction means that one cannot drive from north to south straight through town; you have to jog at Fifth Street, the correction line.

On the way to Fort Dodge there was a major windmill farm off to the left—I'm seeing more and more of these. After stocking up in town, we camped at Bushy Creek Equine Recreation Area, probably the nicest campground (certainly in terms of maintaining the facilities) that we had seen so far. It was nearly empty, but for some campers with their horses some ways off.

October 1—Elberon, Iowa

We left Bushy Creek about 9:30 a.m. and headed off to Waterloo to change Wade's Canadian money. The town was pretty depressing, though you could see it had been something once. The downtown was unbusy, and there were signs that businesses were still moving out. We found a Chinese restaurant—you can always depend on them—and got Wade's money changed at a nearby bank where most of the reading material was in Spanish.

We stopped at a Wal-Mart at the edge of town to make up an 8x10 of a photo of Charlie and Dolores we had taken in Churchill. We framed it as a gift for them and pointed the camper south toward Elberon, where they lived.

Dolores had called my home and left a message, because she wasn't sure when we were arriving. They have a nice, traditional Iowa farmhouse, with about 400 acres. Seemed like a lot to me, but that is not big either by local standards or compared with what they had farmed when they were younger. They gave us a tour of their properties, driving their Jeep over muddy pastures straight at their cows, who gave way at the last moment. The tour took us through Chelsea, which had been flooded out, so the authorities were trying to get everyone to move to higher ground with enticements of free land.

Next to Vining, where Dolores was born. The Veselys are Czech and had been active in the local chapter of the Czech Society of America. Until recently Dolores had been the honcho for the annual Testicle Festival in Vining (which had something to do with certain special cuts of meat, and attracted a pretty good crowd). Like so many older social organizations, as one group of spark plugs grew older, there was a shortage of young ones to replace them. Ask the Elks.

Dolores served us dinner of minute steak and mashed potatoes, with some delicious peach pie for dessert. After dinner their son Don and his wife dropped by and watched as Charlie and Dolores taught us a dice game called left–right–center. I won twice; Wade won once. Pure luck with no skill involved (obviously).

October 2—Amana

Dolores got up and made us SOS for breakfast (creamed beef over toast, or "shit on a shingle" in Army speak). I grew to love the stuff when I was in the Army, once I got over the name, but hadn't had it in quite a while. Then Charlie drove us back over to Vining, where we played cards with about 20 of his friends in an old store. Play started with double-deck elimination poker—high hand drops out; last one standing buys coffee. Loser/winners moved over to another table and played Pepper, a game kind of like euchre. This gang had been playing cards with each other for a long time, so frequently they would sort of look at each other and throw in their hands without a card being played. The scorekeeper tallied it all up anyway. Too fast for me. I consider myself something of a card player, but I had no idea what was going on. The finale was a high–low dice game that cost everybody a quarter, with the winner getting the pot.

Back to the farmhouse where Dolores was waiting to join us on a trip to Amana. It is a place I have heard about for years—a communal society that prospered until the Depression, when it became a corporation and made itself famous by turning out refrigerators. I had asked the Veselys about it while we were still in Canada and told them it was a place I had always wanted to see. They suggested several times that it might not be quite what I expected, but once we got to Iowa they insisted on accompanying us.

Amana was not one village, but several. We stopped in the visitors center and watched a film on the community's history. It was a German Lutheran commune that prospered from 1850 until 1930 when a fire in their woolen mill and the Depression combined to upend their economic order. So, they became a corporation and sold appliances—successfully—to the rest of the country. We went to lunch at Ronneburg Restaurant—very good—then walked up and down the main street looking in the shops, as good tourists do. Amana had turned into more of a tourist attraction than anything else. The high point was probably the woolen mills where you could walk around the weaving machines and watch all the moving parts go clickety-clack as they created beautiful fabric patterns.

We drove back to the farm and said goodbye to Charlie and Dolores and hit the road in the driving rain for Keokuk, a place I have heard about for years as sort of the exemplar of America's great middle. We got tired of fighting the weather and pulled into the Sunset Campground outside town. It was a sad old place full of sad old trailers that people were obviously living in—somehow. We were assigned a space, but Wade suddenly changed his mind and we were off in search of someplace else. We ended up at a small state park that we shared with one other trailer, again one that appeared to be permanent. No amenities other than a latrine, but it was only $15.

October 3—Nauvoo

We went back into Keokuk down a main street that was populated with boarded up stores. America's great middle had fallen on hard times. We looked up the local AAA office to ask for information about Nauvoo, Illinois. By now, Wade had connected the dots and deduced that I had a fascination with "new towns." Nauvoo was the Mormon settlement on the Mississippi River that had been their jumping off point for Utah after Joseph Smith was killed. The woman at AAA had apparently been there but had come away with impressions of where to eat and shop and little else. We decided to manage it on our own.

Joseph Smith and the Mormons had always been subjects of fascination for me. When I was in college I had met a pair of the ubiquitous young missionaries who wander the globe in search of converts. Well-scrubbed, earnest, and sincere in their white shirts and name tags, they can be very easy to like, which I'm sure is part of the strategy. It also seems to have a maturing effect on the young men (and some young women these days, too) to be sent off to a strange place to test themselves. Rites of passage have kind of gone out of style in a lot of western cultures, but there is something to them and they are worth another look. Certainly seems to work for the Mormons.

Another source of my fascination is my home's proximity to a Mormon shrine. I live about 9 miles from a spot on the Susquehanna

River where Joseph Smith was supposedly baptized by none other than John the Baptist. There is just a small marker there now, but negotiations have been going on for a while for the church to acquire property rights that would allow it to restore the farm that once stood there, erect a visitors center—the things that would make it a pilgrimage destination and put our rural area on the map, so to speak. So the stop in Nauvoo offered the chance for me to do a little homework about what happened after Smith moved west, and a vision of what might lie in store for my community.

We crossed the Mississippi River and drove up the Illinois side to Nauvoo, which turned out to be much more impressive than I had anticipated. It was once the largest city in Illinois (1850) and the Latter Day Saints have been buying up land (300 acres) to resurrect it. It was sort of a miniature Colonial Williamsburg with restored buildings and a knockout visitors center with several theaters showing different films about the history of the town and Joseph Smith: the first a 15-minute piece on the building and abandoning of Nauvoo; the second on the life story of Joseph Smith from his childhood to his assassination. No mention, Wade pointed out, of Smith's personal army (which is one of the things that caused him to be regarded as a threat by the good citizens of Illinois), polygamy (another thing), or attitudes on race.

These kinds of things preoccupied Wade. One impetus for his religious exploration was the fanaticism that portrays murderous acts such as 9/11 as the virtuous exploits of god's warriors. To strengthen the religious body, focus their minds on some menacing "other," some infidel, that must be resisted and, if possible, overcome. How well it has worked for all kinds of religions, including the fascism of Hitler and the communism of Kim Il Sung (enemies of the people) is a puzzle to Wade, and to me.

A big difference between Nauvoo and Williamsburg is the staffing. Nauvoo is hosted by volunteer couples from around the country who come for 18 months to man (and woman) the desks, do farming and crafts demonstrations, and give oxcart rides. We met Elder Rohrberg, one of the oxcart drivers, who gave us some background on the volunteer program and took us inside the visitors center to meet Elder

Nixon, who arranged for us to see the movies on Nauvoo and Joseph Smith. One of the actors who played in the Nauvoo movie looked just like a friend of mine. I called my friend later to ask if it were her. Her husband said they have been asked this question before. It's not her.

We walked around town taking pictures in front of the restored temple. Then we went to see Elder Rohrberg again, who gave us a ride in the oxcart. [Oxen, by the way, are any castrated male cattle used as draft animals. Did you know that? I thought it was a special breed.] Oxen were preferred for long treks like the one to Salt Lake City, because they could pull harder and longer than horses.

Again, Nauvoo was impressive. It had been the largest city in Illinois in 1850.

Time did not permit us to take side trips to visit some sites that had intrigued me since my college days in West Virginia. One of my closest friends lived in Moundsville, named for the Grave Creek Mound that may have been built a couple of thousand years ago. I told Wade of my fascination with the idea that there were civilized cultures in places around the world much earlier than we had been educated to believe. This was, in some ways, a continuation of our earlier discussion of underwater cities and the great flood. In any case, Wade was unfamiliar with the moundbuilders and was dubious that there could have been organized cities of tens of thousands of people (Cahokia in Illinois is the site of a huge pyramid, was home to as many as 40,000 people, and was just one of many such communities in the Ohio Valley and Southeastern United States).

As I say, we were educated to think differently about pre-European North America, as well as other areas outside Central America and the Andes. Now, however, there is a growing body of opinion that there were city states not just in North America, but in the Amazon basin as well that had disappeared by the time the Europeans came in force. New discoveries of ancient roads and towns in the Amazon are coming along at a pretty good clip. I had read a book that theorized what the New World was like before Columbus that challenged the conventional view that had held sway for centuries (*1491: New Revelations of the Americas Before Columbus*).

It takes time, often a very long time, for such ideas to gain acceptance. The resistance to new ideas and different opinions can get pretty fierce. One of the great puzzles to me is the ferocious certainty so many people display about things they cannot possibly know. Religion is one obvious case in point – obvious to me, anyway. The very fact that there are so many very different religions with so many fervent adherents should raise some doubts. They cannot all be right. This does not seem to trouble the faithful, however. I even know people who have moved from one faith to another several times, without any diminution of their righteous certitude whatsoever.

But there is no need to single out religious beliefs. The same phenomenon holds true in all other areas of human activity. Attempting to put forth a contrarian perspective is likely to be met with scorn and outright hostility, at least until it becomes irrefutable. Bill Bryson in his wonderful book, *A Short History of Nearly Everything*, lays out one instance after another before citing Alexander von Humboldt's axiom on the three stages of scientific discovery: "first, people deny that it is true; then they deny that it is important; finally, they credit the wrong person."

We had lunch at Grandpa John's and then drove across Illinois to Watseka, where I guessed wrong on diners (again) and had one of the worst meals yet. We camped at the Caboose RV Camp on a lake at the crossroads of two interstates near Remington, Indiana. Noisy, but otherwise okay.

October 4—Indiana

We drove on into Indiana, stopping at Peru (pronounced PeeRoo by the locals, and like the country by everyone else). I knew that it was the home of Cole Porter and, being an amateur songwriter myself, could not pass Cole's home without stopping in. The museum on the main street had an exhibit of his memorabilia, including the Cadillac he shipped to Europe when he traveled there. It cost $6800 new and $180,000 to restore. No statue of Cole I could pose beside, or of Ole Oleson or Tom Mix, two other celebrities from these parts.

I had not realized that Peru also had a celebrated circus museum, a couple of them actually, but most notably the International Circus Hall of Fame. I have a friend who is a circus crazy, so I picked up some souvenirs for him.

On to Decatur, home of Dan Quayle—it says so on the sign coming into town. There is even a Dan Quayle museum. Time did not permit....

Lunched at a Bob Evans, camped in Randolph, Ohio.

October 5—Ohio and Home

The last leg. And the first one where we had run into significant traffic since our first day on the road, coincidentally also in Ohio. We passed by Finley, where they had just had incredible floods. Wade said that Ohio looked a lot like Virginia: light gray soil, rolling hills, and plenty of trees.

On into Pennsylvania where we headed north and took the northern Route 6 most of the way across the state. That took us through a charming town, Franklin, on the day they were having their apple festival. The town was packed.

Also through Tionesta, where someone had built a new lighthouse, just because he liked lighthouses. As near as we could tell it served no useful purpose but to attract attention.

Coming into Coudersport, we saw a huge new building in pseudo-classic style with a big sign saying it is to be auctioned off. It looked completely out of place, as if Nero had decided to build his palace in Mayberry. Then I remembered that this was the home of Adelphia Communications, which was involved in a big financial scandal and filed for bankruptcy.

We made our last side trip to see the Grand Canyon of Pennsylvania, which Wade had never heard of. I myself was unaware of it until I had moved to Pennsylvania. It is 1400 feet deep, and, unlike its namesake in Arizona, covered with trees from top to bottom. It was a bright sunny day, and the trees were arrayed in full fall regalia, which probably explains the crowded parking lots. Obviously there were many people who, unlike me, knew all about it.

EPILOGUE

Wade dropped me off in New Milford and hung around for a day or two, partly to talk to a friend of mine who had made the kind of cross country bike trip that Wade was thinking about. We would spend the following days reflecting—reflecting on the trip just completed and the one coming up...whenever.

In the Army we had names for these exercises: after action reports; lessons learned.

Wade set to work almost immediately organizing his reflections into bests and worsts; calibrating the experience, if you will (did I mention he was an engineer?). He also informed me that we had traveled 6961 miles (not counting the train ride) and burned 493 gallons of gas for an average mpg of 14.0990559445517. He actually prepared a chart that catalogued each leg of the trip with details on odometer readings, number of gallons, miles per gallon for that leg, cost, etc. (Now do you believe he's an engineer?)

What would we do differently? Well, we know we didn't take enough pictures. Next time we should photograph all the interesting people we meet along the way. And, we should spend more time with them. Wade ranks the couple of days we spent with the Veselys as one of the high points of the trip, and I agree. If we did it again, we would slow down a little, drive less and talk more.

But, hey, life is a journey and journeys are time to learn. And that never changes, whether you are a 6-year-old kid on a school field trip, or two 60-something old Army buddies on a road trip. We still have a lot to learn.

And there will always be next time.

Bibliography

Bryson, Bill, *A Short History of Nearly Everything* (New York: Random House-Broadway Books, 2003), 544pp.

Hancock, Graham, *Underworld The Mysterious Origins of Civilization* (New York: Crown Publishers, 2002), 760pp.

Jenkins, Peter, *A Walk Across America* (HarperCollins Publishers, 2001) 320 pp.

Kerouac, Jack, *On the Road* (Viking Penguin 2002) 352pp.

Least Heat-Moon, William, *Blue Highways: A Journey into America* (Little, Brown & Co, 1982) 448 pp.

Lewis, C.S., *Surprised by Joy: The Shape of My Early Life* (Harcourt, 1995) 230 pp.

Mann, Charles C., *1491: New Revelations of the Americas Before Columbus*, (Knopf 2005) 560 pp.

McMurtry, Larry, *Roads: A Millennial Journey Along America's Great Interstate Highways* (Simon & Schuster 2001) 208 pp.

Steinbeck, John, ***Travels with Charley in Search of America*** (Viking, 1980)

Stewart Rory, ***The Places In Between***, (Harcourt, 2006) 298 pp.

Waugh, Evelyn, ***When the Going Was Good***, (Little, Brown & Co., 1985) 298 pp.

ABOUT THE AUTHOR:

John Reynolds is a free-lance writer who specializes in business writing about insurance and finance. He wanders into nonfiction, children's writing and song lyrics when time permits. John lives in New Milford, PA.